THE
WELL DOG
BOOK

THE
WELL DOG
BOOK

Terri McGinnis D.V.M.
author of THE WELL CAT BOOK

illustrated by
Tom Reed D.V.M.

A RANDOM HOUSE • BOOKWORKS BOOK

First printing, August 1974   10,000 copies in cloth
Second printing, February 1975   2,500 copies in cloth
Third printing, June 1975   5,000 copies in cloth
Fourth printing, October 1975   5,000 copies in cloth
Fifth printing, March 1976   5,000 copies in cloth
Sixth printing, December 1976   5,000 copies in cloth
Seventh printing, October 1977   5,000 copies in cloth

Illustrations by Tom Reed, D.V.M.
Typeset by Vera Allen Composition Service, Hayward, California
  (With special thanks to Dorothy, Vera and Paul)
Printed and bound under the supervision of Dean Ragland,
  Random House
Photos by John Pearson

This book is co-published by Random House Inc
                             201 East 50th Street
                             New York N Y 10022

                        and The Bookworks
                             628 Vincente Avenue
                             Berkeley, California 94707

Distributed in the United States by Random House and simultaneously
published in Canada by Random House of Canada Ltd, Toronto.

Booksellers please order from Random House Inc.

Library of Congress Cataloging in Publication Data

McGinnis, Terri.
    The well dog book.

    "A Random House/Bookworks book."
    1. Dogs.   2. Dogs—Diseases.   I. Title.
SF427.M184   636.7'98'96024   74-7496
ISBN 0-394-48948-9

Manufactured in the United States of America

To Wilda,
who never said
*"Little girls don't grow up
to be veterinarians."*

How To Use This Book
For Quick Reference

TO UNDERSTAND
> your dog's body, turn to page 7.

TO FIND INFORMATION
> about daily dog care, turn to page 39.

FOR HELP DIAGNOSING
> the signs of illness or injury, turn to page 95.

IN AN EMERGENCY SITUATION,
> turn to page 144.

FOR HELP GIVING MEDICATION,
> turn to page 169.

FOR SOLUTIONS TO PROBLEMS
> of breeding and reproduction, turn to page 187.

Table of Contents

Introducing the Well Dog

This book is different from other books on dog care because it shows you how to understand the signs of illness or injury your dog may develop and how to evaluate those signs in order to begin proper treatment. In some cases you are advised to seek a veterinarian's help. In others you are advised how you can pursue home treatment. Therefore this book is a kind of paramedic's manual for dogs, standing halfway between the healthy dog and the need for a veterinarian's skill. It should help save you money wasted in unnecessary veterinary visits.

Using this book will help you learn to use your veterinarian as a resource. It is not intended as a substitute for visits to the veterinarian, but rather as a supplement to them. Show this book to your veterinarian as a sign that you are interested in taking an active part in preserving your dog's health.

This book will help you get to know your dog's body better — what is normal and what isn't normal about it. It will help you understand what your veterinarian is talking about when your dog's health is discussed, enable you to treat some illnesses at home, prevent others, and enable you to truly help your veterinarian get your dog well when the illness is too severe to be treated without professional skills. I've tried to include those basic things I wanted most to know as a dog owner before I became a veterinarian, and I've tried to answer the questions dog owners most often ask me about dog health care. I've tried not to oversimplify things, but in many cases technical information I thought the average dog owner would not be interested in is not included.

1

Only *common* problems are covered. If you are interested in details on certain subjects, go to some of the references mentioned or ask your veterinarian for titles of books that might help you.

You don't need to buy any specialized equipment to use this book. Your eyes, hands, ears, and nose, and an understanding relationship with your dog are your most important tools. Don't be afraid to use them. There are more similarities between dogs and people than many dog owners realize. As you read, you will probably find out that you know a lot more about "dog medicine" than you think you do.

The best way to use this book is to read it through at least once from beginning to end. In this way you will learn what is normal and how to take care of a healthy dog, then the things that can indicate illness and what you should do about them. With this first reading you will find out which sections of the book you would like to read again and which sections you will only need to refer to if a specific problem arises. If you want to use this book to learn about a specific problem your dog may have now, look for the problem in the General Index (page 225) and in the Index of Signs (page 100). To learn how to use these indices, see page 95.

Anatomy is the place to begin. With this section as a guide you will learn a ready familiarity with your dog's body. You may wish to refer back to this section when diagnosing signs as well.

Preventive Medicine is a general health care section covering important aspects of the daily life of your dog. It and the following sections have been designed for easy frequent reference by the use of running titles in the margins.

Diagnostic Medicine is the heart of the book. Be sure to read enough of this section to understand how it is organized and how to use the Index of Signs. Then, when your dog shows a sign of illness or injury, use this section as a guide to your action.

Home Medical Care tells you the basics of home treatment. It includes general nursing procedures and advice on drugs. Since in most cases of illness or injury your dog will have some treatment at home, you may want to become familiar with the information in it before beginning to diagnose signs.

Breeding and Reproduction contains facts about the dog's reproductive cycle. Use it to learn how to prevent or plan pregnancy, how to care for a female before, during and after birth, and how to care for newborn or orphan puppies.

You, Your Dog and Your Veterinarian will help you if you don't yet have a veterinarian or are dissatisfied with your present one. Use it to learn what I think are characteristics of good veterinarians and what I think most veterinarians like to see in their clients.

The body always tries to heal itself. This important fact will help your treatment when your dog is sick. In many cases you will not need veterinary aid. Remember though, that by electing to treat your dog at home, you are taking responsibility for the results. Learn to recognize when the body is losing the battle to heal itself. If you can't be *sure* you are really helping your dog, discuss the problem with a doctor of veterinary medicine. Another caution: medicine is not always black or white. There are several equally good ways to approach most health problems. I've recommended the approach that works for me; your veterinarian may disagree and get equal success with other methods. Trust your veterinarian and your common sense.

In several places throughout this book you will come across what seem to be unusual uses of the pronouns they, their, *and* them. *These words have been chosen to avoid the use of gendered pronouns when referring to an indefinite person.*

Anatomy —
Getting to Know Your Dog's Body

Muscle and Bone
Skin
Eyes
Ears
Digestive System
Reproductive and Urinary Organs
Heart and Blood
Respiratory System
Nervous and Endocrine Systems

Physical Examination

Physical examination consists of applying knowledge of anatomy in a routine and thorough inspection of all or part of your dog's body. Each person (including every veterinarian) develops their own method for giving a physical examination. The best routine to develop is one which prevents you from forgetting to examine any part and one with which you feel most comfortable.

Example: Examine your dog by systems as set out in *Anatomy* (muscle and bone, digestive system, etc.). Then return to examine miscellaneous items such as eyes, ears, and lymph nodes. Then take the dog's temperature.

Example: Take the dog's temperature. Proceed with examination starting with the head and working towards the tail. In addition to examining special structures in the area, e.g., ears, eyes, mouth and nose for the head, toenails and pads for the limbs, don't forget to examine the skin in each area and to look for the lymph nodes associated with each area. Follow up by watching your dog in motion.

Special tools needed for physical examination: A rectal thermometer is the only special tool necessary for performing a routine physical examination of your dog at home. Your other tools are your five senses, particularly the senses of touch, sight, and smell.

Special terms used in physical examination: Except for anatomical names of body parts which are mentioned and illustrated in *Anatomy,* there are few special terms that you need to learn to help you with a physical examination. Refer to this page if any of the following words are confusing in the text:

palpate — to examine with your hands. This is one of your most important methods of physical examination and is why you are asked to *palpate* or *feel* parts of your dog's body so frequently throughout this book.

Terms which indicate direction in reference to the body are illustrated below.

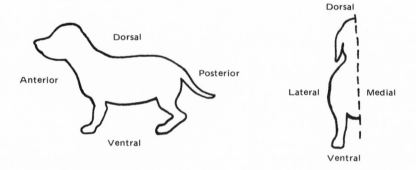

Anatomy

You can't do a good job of giving your dog health care at home without some basic knowledge of *anatomy* and *physiology*. *Anatomy* is the structure of your dog's body and the relationships between its parts. For example, knowing the location of your dog's eyes and ears and their normal appearance is knowing anatomy. *Physiology* is the knowledge of how the parts of your dog's body function. Understanding how your dog's eyes and ears function to enable your dog to see and hear is an example of understanding physiology. Although you will be able to examine and understand anatomy, physiology is much more difficult. Brief descriptions of how your dog's various parts work are given here, but it takes intensive study such as your veterinarian has given the subject to really understand animal physiology well.

You will be most concerned with the external anatomy of your dog, but I've included some internal anatomy as well since an introduction to it will help you understand your veterinarian more easily as you discuss health problems your dog may have. The easiest and fastest way for you to become familiar with what you need to know is to get together with your dog and the following pages. Handle your dog as you read the descriptions and look at the drawings. If you have a puppy, you should examine them several times as they grow. You will see many changes over several months, and the physical contact will bring you closer to one another.

Looking carefully at your dog's anatomy and making your dog sit quietly while you examine them are extremely important in preparing yourself and your dog for times when you will have to give health care at home. Also, the maneuvers you go through in examining your dog at home are the same ones your veterinarian uses when they give your dog a physical exam. A dog who has become accustomed to such handling at home is more relaxed and cooperative at the veterinary office.

If your dog squirms as you try to examine them, tell them "No!" sharply and firmly, reassure them, and once they are still, begin again. Every time they wiggle correct them, and every time they cooperate be sure to reward them with praise and petting. DO NOT give up if your dog wiggles away. It is not too much to ask them to stand, sit or lie calmly as you touch them. (Puppies under four or five months of age seem to have shorter attention spans, so limit your exams with them to five minutes or so.) If your dog is very uncooperative or very small you may find that placing them on a smooth surfaced table enables you to examine them more easily.

Muscle and Bone
(The *Musculoskeletal* System)

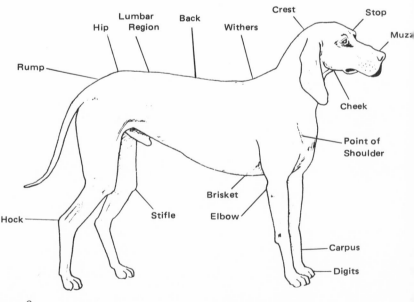

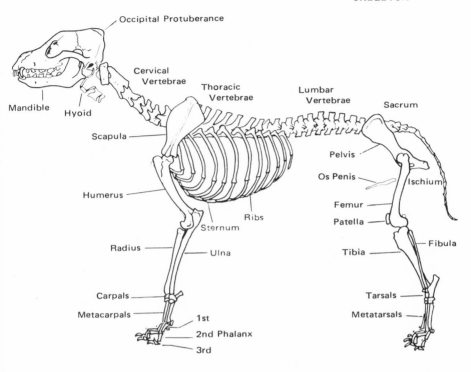

Muscle tissue is composed of contractile units which provide the power for voluntary movement, breathing, blood circulation, digestion, glandular secretion and excretion of body wastes, as well as many other more minor functions. There are three types of muscle tissue in your dog's body. *Smooth* or *unstriated* is involved in a host of primarily involuntary body functions such as the *peristaltic* (wave-like) movements of the digestive tract. *Cardiac* (heart) muscle, which is capable of independent rhythmic contraction, is found *only* in the heart, the pump of the circulatory system. *Skeletal* or *striated* muscle makes up the rest of the muscles in the body, including the diaphragm and certain trunk muscles responsible for breathing. An illustration of the muscles in your dog's body and their names is not included in this book because such knowledge is not important for dog health care at home.

9

Bone is a continually changing and actively metabolizing tissue in the living animal. It is composed primarily of the minerals calcium and phosphorus in an organic connective tissue framework which is mainly protein. The outstanding physical functions of bone are to form the *skeleton* which supports and protects the *soft tissues* (organs, muscle, fat) of the body, and to provide levers against which the various skeletal muscles move. The bones have other functions as well: mineral storage is provided in the hard bone itself, and fat storage and the formation of blood cells occur in the marrow present inside the bones.

Cartilage

CUT-AWAY VIEW OF LONG BONE

Marrow Cavity

Cortex

The "average" dog has 319 bones in their skeletal structure. Names of bones which might be important to you in understanding your veterinarian are marked on the skeletal drawing. See whether you can locate each of them with your hands.

Start with the *skull* (head). Thick and thin layers of muscle and connective tissue overlie the bones of the skull. You can feel the thick, paired *temporal* muscles covering the top of the head. Feel the bony area between these muscles and trace it back to its end behind the ears. This hard bump at the end is called the *occipital protuberance* and is a normal part of every dog's skull. It is more prominent in some breeds (e.g., Irish setters) than others. The *masseter* muscles are another set of easily felt muscles on your dog's head. They form the cheeks and with the temporal and other smaller muscles help close the mouth. The rest of the skull feels very bony; in fact, in very small breeds of dogs you may have difficulty feeling any muscles at all. The *mandible* forms the dog's lower jaw. Move this bone by opening and closing your dog's mouth (see page 24).

The skull is attached to the rest of the skeleton by the *cervical vertebrae.* Try to feel these neck bones by moving your fingers firmly over the sides and top of the neck. You

10

will find it very difficult to feel any bony structures because of the well-developed muscles which cover the neck. The cervical vertebrae along with the other vertebrae form your dog's *spinal column* (backbone).

The *thoracic vertebrae* start in the area between the edges of the shoulder blades. You can feel the curved upper edge of each *scapula* (shoulder blade) near the middle of the back at the *withers*. Each scapula and the muscles which cover it can be seen and felt to move freely when your dog walks or runs. Unless your dog is fat you will be able to feel the spines of the thoracic vertebrae between the shoulder blades. Use your fingers to trace these bones down the center of your dog's back. They become the spines of the *lumbar vertebrae* in the area behind the last rib and disappear near the hip where several vertebrae are joined to form the *sacrum*. You can feel only the spines (end points) of the vertebral bones and not the rest of them because a heavy group of muscles lies on each side of the spinal column. Feel these *epaxial* muscles by running your fingers along each side of the bony spines. If your dog has a tail, you may be able to feel each *coccygeal* (tail) vertebrae under its covering muscles.

Now examine each leg starting with the feet. The "standard dog" has five *digits* (toes) on each front foot. The first, commonly called the *dewclaw,* is rudimentary and does not touch the ground. It is often removed a few days after birth to meet breed standards, and, in working dogs in particular, to avoid tearing caused by snags. Your dog may or may not have a first digit present on each hind foot, but it is commonly present in larger breeds. In fact, some, like Great Pyrenees, have two. Feel each toe carefully. You will see that each consists of three bones *(phalanges).* These correspond to the bones in your fingers and toes. Each toe is attached to a long bone which corresponds to the bones that form the palm of your hand and the sole of your foot. These bones are called *metacarpals* in the front feet and *metatarsals* in the rear.

The front foot *(forepaw)* attaches to the *foreleg* (front leg) at the *carpus* (wrist). Flex and extend this joint. If you *palpate* (examine with your hands) carefully, you may be able to feel the individual bones which form this joint. Above the carpus are the long bones of the *forearm,* the *radius* and *ulna.* These bones are well covered by muscles on the outside *(lateral)* surface except in the region of the elbow. On the *medial* (inside) surface you can feel bone (the radius) near the wrist. Cup the palm of one hand over the elbow. (In small dogs, place the fingers of one hand over it.) Grasp the forearm with your other hand and flex and extend the joint. A normal joint moves smoothly causing no grating or grinding vibrations in your palm. The *humerus* is the bone which forms the foreleg above the elbow. It is well covered with muscles that correspond to those in your upper arm. The humerus is easy to feel at the point of the shoulder; in other areas you will only be able to feel it as a firm structure underlying the muscles.

In the *hindlimb* (rear leg) the foot attaches to the leg at the *hock.* This joint corresponds to your ankle. Flex and extend this joint to learn its normal movement. The fibrous band which attaches prominently on the posterior surface of the hock is the "Achilles tendon." It is part of a mechanism which causes the hock to flex or extend whenever the *stifle* (knee) is flexed or extended and vice versa. The *tibia* and *fibula* are the bones which lie between the knee and the hock. Muscles cover the lateral surface of these bones but you can easily feel the tibia on the inside surface of the leg in this area. These bones join with the *femur* to form the stifle joint. The *patella* (kneecap) is also an important part of this joint. Cup the palm of one hand over the patella (in small dogs place the fingers of one hand over it) and

REAR LEG

Femur

Gastrocnemius Muscle

Patella

Fibula

Tibia

Achilles Tendon

EXAMINING THE JOINT

12

flex and extend the knee joint. You should be able to feel the patella move freely and smoothly as you manipulate the joint. Now move up the leg to the *thigh.* The femur is the long bone of the thigh. It is well covered by heavy muscles so you will be unable to feel it except near the knee. Feel the muscles of the thigh and try to feel the femur under them. The femur *articulates* (forms a joint) with the *pelvis* at the hip. To test this joint, place the palm of your hand against the hip and flex and extend the joint. You can do this either with your dog standing on three legs or lying on one side.

Complete your examination of the musculoskeletal system by running your fingers over the sides of your dog's chest. You should be able to feel each rib easily under a freely moveable coat of skin, fat and muscle. If you can't easily feel the ribs, your dog is too fat. Pick a rib and follow it with your fingers down the side of the *thorax* (chest) to its end. If you have chosen one of the first nine ribs you will find that it attaches to a bone forming the *ventral* (bottom) surface of the chest. This is the *sternum.* The last four ribs do not attach directly to the sternum.

If you have a male dog another bone to notice is the *os penis.* This bone is present inside the penis of the male dog. The urethra passes through it. An equivalent structure is not usually present in the clitoris of the female dog.

After you have examined the major parts of your dog's musculoskeletal system (or before, if you like), stand back and look at your dog as a whole. Are the legs straight? Are the wrist joints erect? Are there any unusual lumps or bumps? Some breeds, such as basset hounds and bulldogs, have certain essentially abnormal types of *conformation* (bony and muscular structure) bred into them and seem to function well in spite of anatomy that would be considered abnormal in other dogs. Most normal dogs, however, are similar in structure to the drawings in this book.

Now watch your dog move. All motion should be free and effortless. Do you see any signs of lameness? If you have any particular questions about your dog's conformation or gait be sure to discuss them with your veterinarian.

Skin
(The *Integumentary* System)

The integumentary system consists of the skin and its specialized modifications, the hair, the footpads, claws and anal sacs. Your dog's skin protects their body against environmental changes, trauma and germs. In the skin vitamin D is synthesized; below the skin (in the *subcutaneous* tissues) fat is stored. Skin is both an organ of sensation and an organ (via certain skin glands) for waste excretion. Unlike in humans, however, the dog's body skin plays only a minor role in heat regulation. Skin disease is a common problem in dogs, and the condition of your dog's skin can sometimes tell you a great deal about their body's general state of health.

If your dog is healthy, their skin should be smooth, pliable and free from large amounts of scales (dandruff), scabs, odorous secretions and parasites (see page 83). Normal skin color ranges from pale pink through shades of brown to black. Spotted skin is completely normal and may be seen in dogs without spotted coats. The skin (and hair) color comes from a dark-colored pigment called *melanin* which is produced and stored in special cells in the bottom layer of the *epidermis* (outer skin layer).

Examine your dog's skin carefully. To do this, part the fur of long-haired dogs in several places and look carefully at the skin itself. In short-haired dogs, run the thumb of one hand against the grain of the hair to expose the skin. Be sure to examine the skin in several places over the body, on the legs, under the neck and on the head. Any bug-like creatures you see attached to your dog's skin or hair or which quickly move away as you part the hair are *external parasites* and should not be there. They are likely to be ticks (see page 86), lice (see page 87), or fleas (see page 83). Small salt and pepper-like, black and white granules present may be flea eggs and flea feces.

Roll your dog on their back to see where the skin forms the nipples of the *mammary glands* (breasts). The mammary glands themselves are skin glands which have become modified for the production of milk. Male as well as female dogs normally have five nipples on each side, although the number may vary from four to six. The prominence of the nipples and mammary glands in the female varies with age and stage of the *estrous cycle* (see page 187). Examine your dog's mammary glands by feeling the areas between the nipples and a wide area around them. In a normal male or *anestrous* female (see page 187) you should not be able to feel any lumps or bumps. If you find *any* discuss their importance with your veterinarian.

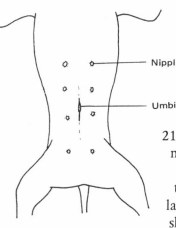

VENTRAL ABDOMEN

Nipple

Umbilicus

While you are examining the breasts, you may notice a scar-like area of skin on the midline near the area where the chest meets the abdomen (belly). This is your dog's *umbilicus* (belly button). If you see a lump in this area, it may be an *umbilical hernia* (see page 210 and decide whether or not you need a veterinarian's help).

The skin is modified over the nose so that its superficial layers are thick and tough. This skin has no glands, but is usually moist from nasal secretions and feels cool as a result. A cool moist nose or a warm dry one, however, is not an accurate gauge of your dog's body temperature; use a thermometer! Most dogs' noses are darkly pigmented, but brown to pink or spotted nose color is normal for some dogs.

The skin is also modified to be thick and tough over the footpads. The deepest layer of the footpads is very fatty and acts as a cushion to absorb shock. The middle layer *(dermis)* contains *eccrine glands:* the only skin glands in the dog equivalent to humans' heat-regulating sweat glands. On warm days you may see your dog leave steamy footprints on the pavement from the eccrine gland secretion.

The footpads are named according

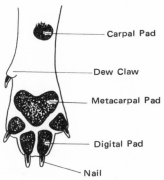

FRONT PAW

Carpal Pad

Dew Claw

Metacarpal Pad

Digital Pad

Nail

15

to which bones they overlie — *digital, metacarpal (metatarsal* on the rear feet), and *carpal* (none on the rear feet). Examine your dog's footpads and learn their names. Knowing the names may help you describe the location of a problem to your veterinarian.

Two unusual modifications of skin are the *anal sacs*. The anal sacs are located internally under the external sphincter muscles of the anus at about the three o'clock and nine o'clock positions. The duct of each sac empties just inside the anus. With some practice, you can feel the full sacs by placing your thumb externally on one side of the anus and your index finger on the other side, then gently moving your fingers up and down. When full, each sac varies from about the size of a pea in very small dogs to the size of a Concord grape in large dogs. The anal sac glands produce a sour to rancid smelling, thick secretion which may serve to mark your dog's stool with their particular identification tag. The sacs are often emptied explosively in stressful or frightening situations. Occasionally a dog's anal sacs don't empty properly on their own; then you or your veterinarian must empty them (see page 137).

ANAL SACS

Anus
Duct
Anal
Sac

Claws (toenails) are epidermis special-ized for digging and traction. The outer layer of the claw is horny and may be pigmented, partially pigmented, or unpig-mented. The inner layer is the *dermis* (quick) which contains many blood vessels and is continuous with the connective tissue covering the third phalanx. If your

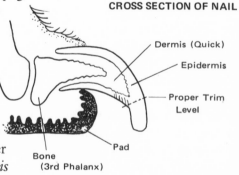

CROSS SECTION OF NAIL

Dermis (Quick)
Epidermis
Proper Trim Level
Pad
Bone
(3rd Phalanx)

dog has light-colored nails, you can see the dermis as a pink area inside the claw when it is held in front of a light. Normal claws just touch the ground, allowing the foot to stand compactly. Excessively long nails cause the foot to *splay* (spread out abnormally) and make walking uncomfortable and the gait unnatural. If some dogs' nails are neglected too long, they grow

HEALTHY FOOT

OVERGROWN NAILS

out, around and into the digital pads causing pain and sometimes infection. Be sure to check your dog's toenails now and repeat the examination frequently to prevent them from becoming too long. To learn how to cut your dog's toenails properly see page 50.

Dogs have three basic types of hair: guard hair, fine hair, and tactile hair. *Tactile hairs* (whiskers) grow out of very large sensory hair follicles on the muzzle and chin, at the sides of the face, and over the eyes. Their sensory function may be of particular importance in helping your dog orient themself in poor light. Wild *canids,* such as wolves, and domestic dogs with wild type coats, such as German shepherds, have both guard hairs and fine hairs covering their bodies. *Guard hairs* are the longer, coarser hairs. *Fine hairs* comprise the undercoat. In other breeds one or the other type of hair usually predominates. For example, the boxer has a coat of fine, short hairs, the poodle a coarse (wooly), long coat. Other classifications of hair types in dogs have been made but are unimportant for our purposes. Try to determine which kind of hair your dog has.

All dogs are replacing their coats continuously. At any one time some hairs are falling out, some are in a resting phase, and others are growing in. You may notice a particular increase in the number of hairs your dog sheds in the spring and again in the fall, but there is no reason to consider your dog shedding excessively unless you begin to see bare skin areas developing. Your dog's coat should appear glossy and unbroken. Dark-colored coats usually seem to have more natural sheen, so take this into consideration before judging your dog's coat, especially if it is a light-colored one. After clipping or shaving, the average dog's coat takes three to four months to regrow. Long coats may take more than a year.

Eyes

Your dog's eyes are similar in structure and function to your own. Light entering the eye passes through the cornea, anterior chamber, pupil, lens, and vitreous body before striking the retina. Specialized cells in the retina (the rods and cones) convert light striking

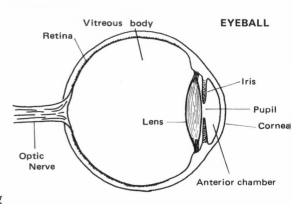

EYEBALL

them into nervous signals which pass via the optic nerve to the brain. In dogs these impulses result in an image thought to be perceived in various shades of gray *(color blindness)* and degrees of brightness.

  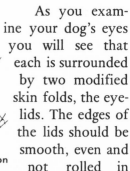

Normal Eye Lids   Entropion   Ectropion

As you examine your dog's eyes you will see that each is surrounded by two modified skin folds, the eyelids. The edges of the lids should be smooth, even and not rolled in *(entropion)* or out *(ectropion)*. The margin of the upper lid has well-developed eyelashes. Look carefully for lashes which grow abnormally so that they rub against the eye, and look for fine lashes which may form an abnormal extra row. Such lashes can be very irritating and must often be removed. Between the lids at the *medial canthus* (edge of the eye near

18

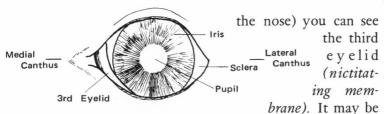

Medial Canthus

Iris

Lateral Canthus

Sclera

Pupil

3rd Eyelid

EXTERNAL EYE

the nose) you can see the third eyelid (*nictitating membrane*). It may be pale pink or pigmented, and its normal position over the eye varies from dog to dog. Roll back the upper or lower eyelid by placing your thumb near its edge and gently pulling upward or downward. This allows you to view the inner lining of the lids, a pale pink mucous membrane called the *conjunctiva*.

EXAMINING THE EYE

Swollen 3rd Eyelid

Inflamed Sclera

Conjunctiva

(Forms Conjunctival Sac when lid released)

The visible part of the eyeball consists of the cornea, bulbar conjunctiva, anterior chamber, iris and pupil. The *bulbar conjunctiva* is a continuation of the lining of the eyelids. If it contains pigment, the area may look spotted or dark. In unpigmented areas the bulbar conjunctiva is transparent, allowing the eye's white fibrous coat (*sclera*) and the fine blood vessels which traverse it to be seen through it. The cornea should be completely transparent. Through it you see the anterior chamber, iris and pupil. In most dogs the iris is colored dark to golden brown; however, in some dogs (e.g., Old English sheep dog) it is light blue or spotted. The iris controls the size and shape of the pupil. Along with the eyelids, the pupil controls the amount of light allowed to enter the eye. Pupils should constrict simultaneously in bright light and dilate in dim light. When only one eye is exposed to light or darkness, the pupil of the remaining eye should constrict or dilate when the exposed one does. The pupils of dogs' eyes are normally round in shape; see if your dog's are when you test their response to light.

19

Ears

Whether your dog's ears stand up, partially flop over, or hang completely down, their anatomy is basically the same. The external part of the ear, which you can see when casually looking at your dog, is called the *pinna*. The pinna receives air vibrations and transmits them via the ear canal to the eardrum. If your dog has non-erect ears, you can make an ear correspond to the illustration by grasping the tip of the pinna and lifting it straight up.

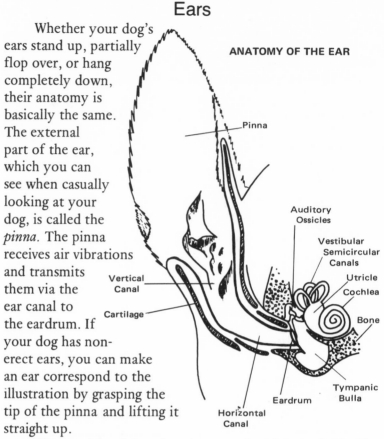

ANATOMY OF THE EAR

Pinna

Auditory Ossicles

Vestibular Semicircular Canals

Utricle

Cochlea

Vertical Canal

Bone

Cartilage

Tympanic Bulla

Eardrum

Horizontal Canal

The outside of the pinna is covered with haired skin like that covering the rest of your dog's body. The inside is also partially haired, although the hair here is usually more sparse than that on the outside. Any visible unpigmented skin lining the inside of the pinna and ear canal should be pale pink in color. Bright pink or red is abnormal. All visible parts of the ear should be fairly clean. Normal accumulations consist of a small amount of brown to black waxy material. Large amounts of this material, waxy orange material, or sticky, foul-smelling secretions are abnormal. If your dog's ears look normal to you, or if your veterinarian tells you that your dog's ears are normal, smell them. This odor is the smell of a healthy ear. Deviations from this smell may indicate ear trouble even if you can't see any external indication of it.

Notice on the drawing that the ear canal is vertical for a distance, then becomes horizontal before it reaches the eardrum. This makes it impossible for you or your veterinarian to see very deeply into the ear canal without a special instrument called an otoscope. An advantage of this type of ear canal structure is that it allows you to clean quite deeply into the ear canal without fear of damaging the eardrum as long as you clean vertically (see page 49).

The structure and function of your dog's middle and inner ear are very similar to your own. Vibrations reaching the ear drum are transmitted through the middle ear by small bones, the *auditory ossicles,* to the *oval window.* From the oval window the vibrations enter the inner ear where the *cochlea* converts these mechanical stimuli to nervous impulses which travel to the brain via the auditory nerve. In addition to the cochlea, the *semicircular canals* and *utricle* occupy the inner ear. These organs are important in maintaining the dog's sense of balance.

Digestive System
(The *Gastrointestinal* System)

The digestive system consists of the digestive tube (mouth, pharynx, esophagus, stomach, small and large intestines and anus) and the associated salivary glands, liver and gall bladder, and pancreas. Few of the foodstuffs necessary for growth, life and work enter the body in a form that can be absorbed directly by the intestines and put straight to use by the body. Therefore it is the digestive system's function to convert foodstuffs to absorbable nutrients, using mechanical and chemical means.

Salivary Glands
Pituitary
Larynx
Thyroid
Trachea (windpipe)
Heart
Lungs
Liver
Diaphragm
Adrenal Gland
Stomach
Spleen
Pancreas
Kidney
Colon

21

Anatomically you will be primarily concerned with the beginning and the end of the gastrointestinal tract — the mouth and the anus. The locations of the other structures are indicated on the drawing of internal anatomy. It is difficult to feel the abdominal organs in most dogs because most dogs tense (contract) their abdominal muscles as you begin to feel for the organs. When your dog's stomach is very full you may be able to feel its edge as a doughy mass against the left *anterior* (toward the head) part of the abdomen just behind the last rib. Try it, but don't be disappointed if the stomach is not obvious. You may be able to feel your dog's intestines by grasping your dog's abdomen between your two hands, pressing your fingers towards one another gently, then moving them downward. The intestines will slip through your fingers like strands of wet spaghetti. If the colon contains feces you may be able to feel it as an irregular tube located high in the *posterior* (toward the tail) abdomen parallel to the spine.

Mouth   Many dogs, especially puppies, are reluctant to have their mouths examined for the first time. Don't give up if your dog squirms or pulls away as you start your examination. Make your intentions clear; be firm yet reassuring. Begin the examination by lifting each upper lip individually with the jaws closed. Use one hand to steady your dog's head, if necessary, while examining with the other. This allows you to examine the *buccal* (outer) surfaces of the teeth and gums.

Healthy gums feel firm and have edges so closely applied to the teeth that they

HEALTHY GUMS   **SEVERE GUM DISEASE**

actually look attached to the teeth. They fill the upper part of the spaces between teeth, forming a "V" which you can see between each upper front tooth and its neighbors. (An inverted "V" between the lower teeth.) In unpigmented areas, healthy gums are pink. Red gums or a red line along the lower edge (next to the tooth) of pink gums is abnormal as are very pale pink, yellowish or white gums. Many normal dogs have black or black spotted gums.

22

Dogs teeth are designed for grasping, tearing and shredding. In a normal mouth, the upper front teeth (incisors) just overlap the lower ones. An excessive overlap (overbite) is abnormal, as is a mouth structure in which the lower front teeth extend beyond the upper ones (underbite). A mild overbite or underbite doesn't seem to cause functional problems, and an underbite is considered desirable

OVERBITE   UNDERBITE

for certain breeds such as the bulldog and boxer. Be sure to check your dog's bite and the surface of each tooth. The tooth surface is white in young dogs and gets yellower as the dog ages. A fingernail scraped along tooth surfaces should pick up little debris. Try it. Mushy white stuff that you may scrape off is called *plaque* or *material alba.* This can be removed easily by "brushing" your dogs teeth (see page 52). Hard white, yellow or brown material is *tartar* or *calculus* and must usually be removed by your veterinarian.

Teeth are categorized into four types: incisors (I), canines (C), premolars (P) and molars (M).

Veterinarians use a formula to indicate the number and placement of each kind of tooth in the mouth. A letter indicates the kind of tooth; the numbers placed next to the letter indicate how many of that particular kind of tooth are present in the upper and lower jaw of one-half the mouth.

Incisors
Canine
Premolars
Molars

The average puppy has twenty-eight *deciduous* (baby) teeth arranged in the following manner: Starting at the middle of the front teeth (incisors)

$$\frac{\text{Upper teeth of } \frac{1}{2} \text{ mouth}}{\text{Lower teeth of } \frac{1}{2} \text{ mouth}} = I\frac{3}{3}, C\frac{1}{1}, P\frac{3}{3}$$

23

A puppy has no molars. The appearance of these baby teeth and their replacement by the permanent ones is a convenient way to estimate the age of a young dog (see table page 26).

The average adult dog has forty-two permanent teeth:

$$\frac{\text{Upper teeth of } \frac{1}{2} \text{ mouth}}{\text{Lower teeth of } \frac{1}{2} \text{ mouth}} = I\frac{3}{3}, \ C\frac{1}{1}, \ P\frac{4}{4}, \ M\frac{2}{3};$$

Dogs with short faces (*brachycephalic* dogs) often have fewer teeth due to the shortening of their jaws. They get along fine, though, with the teeth they have. Once a dog's permanent teeth have erupted it is more difficult to use them as a guide to age.

Now examine the inner (*lingual*) surfaces of the teeth, the tongue, and the posterior part of the mouth. To open your dog's mouth, place one hand around the upper part of their muzzle and push inward on the upper lips with your fingers and thumb as if you were trying to push them between the teeth. As your dog starts to open their mouth, use the fingers of your other hand to pull open the lower jaw by pushing downward on the lower incisor teeth. Look inside. You will

OPENING THE MOUTH

see the tongue below, the hard palate above, and the inner teeth surfaces. You can use your fingers to push the tongue to one side or the other to look under it. Using the fingers of the same hand you used to open the lower jaw, press down on the posterior half of the tongue. As you press down, try to move the tongue slightly forward. If

PHARYNX

Hard Palate

Soft Palate

Tonsil

Epiglottis

you do this properly, you will mimic your doctor's use of a tongue depressor, allowing you to see the soft palate as a continuation of the hard palate and the palantine tonsils. Be very careful when examining back of dog's mouth. If there is any resistance withdraw your hand immediately. Dogs' tonsils reside in a pocket (the *tonsilar crypt* or *sinus*) so they aren't easily seen unless they are enlarged.

Tonsils are a type of specialized *lymphoid* tissue (containing many special cells called *lymphocytes*, see page 66) similar to your lymph nodes and to lymph nodes located in other parts of your dog's body. You can feel some lymph nodes of your dog's head in the area located below your dog's ear and behind the cheek where the head attaches to the neck. They are small, firm, smooth-surfaced lumps associated with a larger similar lump. The larger lump is one of the dog's several salivary glands, and the only one you will be able to feel. After you feel the normal salivary gland and its associated lymph nodes and become familiar with them, try to feel the other lymph nodes indicated on the drawing. (You may need your veterinarian's help with this.) When you find one, learn its normal size and shape. Lymph node changes (most commonly enlargement) should alert you to have your dog examined by a veterinarian since they are often a sign of serious infection or other illness.

LYMPH NODES

Mandibular

Prescapular

Axillary

Inguinal

Popliteal

Teeth As A Guide To Your Dog's Age

Age	Teeth Present
Birth	None
3-4 weeks	Deciduous teeth coming in
6 weeks	All deciduous teeth in
4-5 months	Permanent incisors coming in
5-6 months	Permanent canines start to erupt and by end of 6 months in
6-7 months	Last molar in lower jaw (M3) in

Teeth of large breeds of dogs tend to erupt more rapidly than those of small breeds. Some dogs, particularly those of small breeds, tend to retain their baby teeth as the adult ones erupt. These teeth have to be removed by a veterinarian if they are preventing proper adult tooth placement.

After one year, chewing habits, mouth health, and mouth structure make it much more difficult to age a dog by their teeth. As a guide:

1½ years	Cusp worn off lower middle incisor
2½ years	Cusp worn off lower incisor next to middle
3½ years	Cusp worn off upper middle incisor
4½ years	Cusp worn off upper incisor next to middle
5½ years	Wear on last incisors
6 years	Canines becoming blunt

YOUNG DOG'S TEETH
Cusp

Anus   Just about everyone knows that the anus is the specialized terminal portion of the digestive tract through which undigestible material and waste products pass as stool. But some people have questions regarding what constitutes a normal bowel movement. Others are unaware of the anal sacs located in this area.

Most adult dogs have one or two bowel movements daily. The number of bowel movements and the volume of stool passed, however, are very dependent on the amount of undigestible material in the diet. Dogs eating dry food will tend to pass more feces than dogs eating a highly digestible muscle meat, egg and milk product diet, due to the higher fiber content of dry dog food. Normal stools are well formed and generally colored brown, although some diet ingredients may make them darker (charcoal, liver) or lighter (bones). Extremely large volumes of stool, unformed, particularly odorous, or unusually colored stools may indicate digestive tract disease. Be sure to observe your dog's stools several times a week.

Anal sacs have been discussed with the skin; see page 16. If you have not yet examined them, do it now while learning the normal appearance of your dog's anus. You may also want to learn to take your dog's temperature at this time since it should be a routine part of any physical examination and must be taken rectally in dogs (see page 169).

Reproductive and Urinary Organs
(The *Genitourinary* System)

Major portions of the male dog's reproductive system are located externally where they are fairly easy to examine. The *testes* (organs which produce sperm) are located in the *scrotum* (skin pouch containing the testes) at birth and should be easy to feel by six weeks of age. Normally there are two testicles present, each of which feels firm, smooth and relatively oval. If your dog has one or no testicles in his scrotum *(monorchid or cryptorchid)* the condition may need veterinary attention (see page 193). If you palpate carefully, you can feel a small lump protruding off the posterior end of each testicle. This is the tail of the *epididymis,* which stores sperm.

MALE GENITAL ANATOMY

Labels: Anus, Prostate, Urethra, Epididymis, Testicle, Scrotum, Bulbus Glandis, Colon, Ureter, Vas Deferens, Bladder, Os Penis, Penis, Prepuce

There are two ways to examine your dog's penis. First place your fingers on the outside of the *sheath* (skin covering

27

the penis) and feel the penis through it. Near the posterior end you will be able to feel a slight enlargement. This is the *bulbus glandis*. It becomes engorged with blood during copulation, helping to produce the phenomenon known as the "tie" (see page 197). To examine the surface of the penis itself, grasp the penis firmly through the sheath near the testes and gently push it forward as you use you other hand

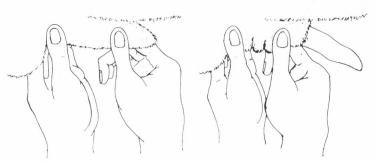

to push the *prepuce* (sheath) back from the anterior portion of the penis. You can maintain the penis in its fully extruded position by placing your index finger between the penis and the abdominal wall with the folds of the prepuce held behind it. The surface of the penis and the inside of the prepuce are normally pink and relatively smooth. In young dogs any secretions present should be clear. In mature males a small amount of cloudy, yellowish discharge is not unusual.

Sperm are produced in the seminiferous tubules of the testicles. From the testis the sperm travels to the epididymis for storage and maturation. During ejaculation sperm travel through the vas deferens into the urethra where they are mixed with secretions from the prostrate gland before exiting the penis. The prostate is located within the abdomen and can be examined only by rectal palpation. If you would like to try to examine your dog's prostate gland, gently insert your gloved and lubricated index finger into the rectum and move it from side to side. (Lightweight disposable gloves can be purchased in drugstores.) As you pass over the prostate, you will feel two lumps joined together. Learn their normal size for your dog, because the prostate size varies between dogs and changes with age.

The vulva and clitoris are the only female dog's genitals which can be seen externally. The internal portions of the female reproductive tract — uterus, cervix, ovaries and fallopian tubes — are illustrated here. The urethra empties into the vagina anterior to a point you can see without special instruments. You can see the clitoris in its

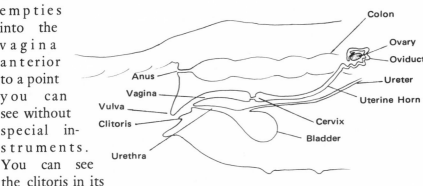

FEMALE GENITAL ANATOMY

Colon
Ovary
Oviduct
Ureter
Uterine Horn
Anus
Vagina
Vulva
Clitoris
Cervix
Bladder
Urethra

fossa by gently pulling the tip of the vulva downward with one hand while spreading the vulvar lips with the other. This also allows you to see some of the lining of the vulva and vagina. These mucous membranes should be pink in color; and any secretions present are normally clear unless the female is in heat.

VULVA

Vaginal Opening
Clitoris

You can find additional information on reproduction in the chapter *Breeding and Reproduction*, page 187.

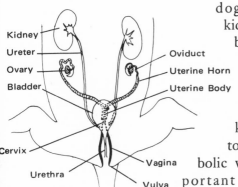

FEMALE GENITAL ORGANS

Kidney
Ureter
Ovary
Bladder
Oviduct
Uterine Horn
Uterine Body
Cervix
Urethra
Vagina
Vulva

The urinary system of both male and female dogs consists of two kidneys, two ureters, the bladder and the urethra. Look for these organs on the illustrations. *Nephrons* (units of specialized cells) in the kidneys filter the blood to remove toxic metabolic wastes and are also important in maintaining the

29

body's proper electrolyte and water balance. Urine formed in the kidneys passes through the ureters to the bladder where it is stored until it is eliminated through the urethra during urination. If your dog's bladder is full or partially full, you may be able to palpate it through the body wall. Feel for a structure similar to a water-filled balloon in the posterior abdomen. Normal urine is yellow and clear. The intensity of the yellow color increases as the amount of water excreted decreases and vice versa. If your dog is small, lean and has a relaxed abdomen, you may be able to feel the kidneys by deep palpation in the lumbar region, but they are more difficult to find than the bladder so don't be disappointed if you aren't successful.

Respiratory System

The dog's respiratory system consists of two lungs, the air passages leading to them (nasal cavity, pharynx, larynx, trachea, bronchi), the diaphragm and the muscles of the thorax. The system's main function, as in humans, is to supply oxygen to the body and to remove excess carbon dioxide produced by metabolism. In conjunction with the tongue and the mucous membranes of the mouth, the respiratory system has a secondary, but extremely important, function of heat regulation in the dog, since the dog has no highly developed mechanism for sweating.

The only parts of your dog's respiratory system you can see are the nostrils and mouth. Special instruments are needed to look into the nasal cavity, and most dogs will not let this area be examined without anesthesia. Look at your dog's nostrils. Any secretions from them should be clear and watery; sticky, cloudy, yellowish or greenish nasal discharges are abnormal.

You can feel your dog's *larynx* (Adam's apple) by grasping their neck on the undersurface where it meets the head. The larynx feels like a hard, fairly inflexible mass. It helps control the flow of air through the trachea and lungs and is the location of the vocal cords responsible for your dog's bark, whine, or howl.

Notice the character of your dog's respirations at rest and after exercise. A normal dog at rest breathes about ten to thirty times per minute. The movements of the chest are smooth and unstrained. After exercise, of course, the rate is much faster and panting may occur. Changes in the rate and character of a dog's respiration may indicate disease. Be sure to become familiar with your dog's normal breathing at rest, on cool and warm days, and during and after exercise so you can tell when changes have occurred.

Heart and Blood
(The *Circulatory* System)

Your dog's circulatory system is similar to your own. It consists of a four-chambered heart which serves as a blood pump, arteries which carry blood away from the heart to the capillaries where molecular exchange occurs, and veins which return blood to the heart. There are no direct methods you can use to examine this system. You could be aided in your examination by the use of a stethoscope, but one is not necessary to deal with everyday health problems you may encounter.

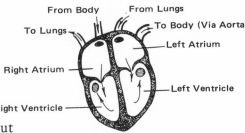

SCHEMATIC DRAWING OF HEART

From Body — From Lungs — To Lungs — To Body (Via Aorta) — Left Atrium — Right Atrium — Left Ventricle — Right Ventricle

The normal heart beats about eighty to one hundred twenty times per minute in the *resting* dog. Small dogs tend to have a more rapid heart rate than large ones. You can feel the heart beat by placing

FEELING THE HEART BEAT

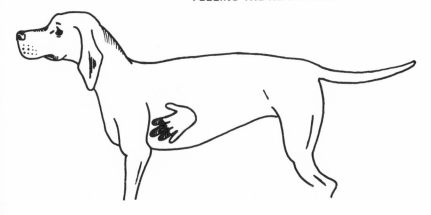

your fingertips or the palm of your hand against your dog's chest just behind the point of the elbow. Many dogs are small enough for you to place your hand completely around the lower part of the chest with your fingers on one side and your thumb on the other. If your dog is very fat you may not be able to feel the heart beat. You can usually hear it though by placing your ear (or a stethoscope) against the chest over the heart. Each heart beat consists of a strong, low-pitched thud followed by a less intense, higher-pitched thud, followed by a pause — lub-dup . . . lub-dup . . . lub-dup.

To take your dog's pulse, place your fingers at the middle of the inside surface of the rear leg near the point where the leg meets the body. This is the area where the femoral artery passes near the skin allowing you to feel the pulse. The heart rate and pulse rate should, of course, be the

FEELING THE PULSE

same. You may notice that they go faster and slower as your dog breathes in and out. This normal variation in rate is called *sinus arrythmia.* It is easiest to count for fifteen seconds, then multiply by four to calculate the rate per minute.

A measure of capillary circulation is *capillary filling time.* To determine this, press one finger firmly against your dog's gums. When you lift it away you will see a pale area which should refill with blood almost instantaneously. This measure of circulation can be helpful in evaluating shock (see page 145).

Blood is the fluid transported by the circulatory system. Blood consists of plasma, platelets, red blood cells and white blood cells. The composition of the liquid portion of the blood, *plasma,* is very complex. It carries nutrients throughout the body, removes wastes, including carbon dioxide, and provides a means of transport for the hormones produced by the endocrine glands, as well as transporting the particulate blood constituents. *Platelets* are produced primarily in the

32

bone marrow of the adult dog. These small bodies help prevent hemorrhage when a blood vessel is injured by aggregating together to form a physical barrier to blood flow and by stimulating clot formation. *Red blood cells* carry oxygen to the tissues and to a much lesser degree transport carbon dioxide away. They give blood its red color. There are several kinds of *white blood cells,* and each type has a particular function. As a group the white cells are most important in preventing and fighting infection.

The *spleen* is an abdominal organ which, although not necessary for life, has many functions related to the blood. In the adult it is a site for the production of some white cells and, in times of need, can produce red cells as well. It is a blood reservoir which can supply large numbers of red cells rapidly when the body needs oxygen. The spleen also removes old and abnormal red blood cells from circulation and stores some red cell components, such as iron.

Nervous and Endocrine Systems

The integration of the functions of the various parts of the body is the function of the nervous system and of the endocrine system. You cannot normally see or feel any of the components of these systems when you examine your dog. Nonetheless, if one system or the other is functioning abnormally it is usually not long before some striking change will occur in your animal. In general the *nervous system* (brain, spinal cord and peripheral nerves) is responsible for rapid body adjustments to environmental and internal stimuli. The *endocrine system* for the most part is responsible for more gradual responses which are mediated by chemical substances *(hormones)* secreted by endocrine glands into the blood stream.

Complete neurological and endocrine examinations are not a routine part of your or your veterinarian's physical exam. For your information a brief outline of the functions of the various endocrine glands are listed on the following page.

Endocrine Gland	Function
Pituitary-Hypothalamus	Regulates the activity of ovaries, testes, thyroid, adrenal cortex. Secretes growth hormone which stimulates growth of body tissues. Controls milk secretion and milk let down. Affects body water balance.
Thyroid	Controls metabolic rate, affects calcium and phosphorus metabolism.
Parathyroids	Influence calcium and phosphorus metabolism.
Adrenals	Cortex: Influences carbohydrate, protein, electrolyte metabolism. Medulla: Secretes adrenalin, noradrenalin which help body prepare for emergencies.
Testes	Influence development of masculine characteristics, influence sex drive.
Ovaries	Influence development of feminine characteristics, influence sexual behavior, estrus, pregnancy.
Islet cells of pancreas	Secrete insulin, glucagon which affect blood sugar level.
Kidney	Renin: Affects blood pressure Erythropoietin: Stimulates red cell production.
Cells of digestive tract	Secrete various hormones which regulate digestive tract motility and secretion of digestive enzymes. Some control over insulin secretion.
Pineal body	Exact function unknown; may affect sexual development and sexual cycles.

Look at the drawings of the internal anatomy to see where these various glands are located. For very detailed information about these glands and other parts of your dog's anatomy and physiology, you may want to consult the following books:

Miller, Malcom E., *Anatomy of the Dog,* W.B. Saunders Company, Philadelphia, Pennsylvania.

Swenson, Melvin J., ed., *Dukes' Physiology of Domestic Animals,* Cornell University Press, Ithaca, New York.

Ganong, W.F., *Review of Medical Physiology,* 6th ed., 1973, Lange Medical Publications, Los Altos, California. (A human physiology text, but the information for the most part applies to dogs.)

Don't be surprised if your first examination of your dog takes an hour or two. If you have a puppy, it may take a full day to complete the exam because you may have to divide it into several parts separated by rest periods to compensate for a puppy's short attention span. Repeat your physical examination at least once a week while you are learning what is normal for your dog. By doing this you will train your dog to cooperate and you will soon find that you no longer need to refer to this book so often. The time it takes for you to perform the examination will shorten considerably as you practice. You should eventually be able to finish it in about fifteen minutes. Most veterinarians become so skilled at physical examination that, until you become aware of what they are doing by reading this book, you may not even realize that a physical examination is being performed. Your veterinarian may easily perform a routine physical in five or ten minutes. Special examinations, of course, take much longer.

Once you are familiar with your dog's anatomy how frequently you repeat certain parts of a physical examination varies. You can get a good idea of your dog's general health and of the health of their muscles and bones daily by just being aware of your dog's appetite and activity. Be sure to examine the ears, eyes, teeth, skin and nails at least every two weeks. And examine the mammary glands of females, in particular, monthly. If your dog lives outside you will probably have to make more of a conscious effort to do the examinations than if you live together inside. If you leave your dog before it is light and return after dark, be sure to set aside time several times a week to study your dog's general condition.

Preventive Medicine —
How to Care for a Healthy Dog

Training
Grooming
Nutrition
Traveling With or Shipping a Dog
Preventive Vaccination Procedures
Internal and External Parasites

Preventive Medicine Calendar

Daily: Feed a balanced diet. See page 53.

Groom dog as demanded by coat type and dog's habits. See page 47.

Observe dog's general external appearance, attitude, activity and appetite. Any change may indicate a need for complete physical examination.

Remove stool from yard or kennel, observe stool and, if possible, also observe the urine.

Weekly: Examine for external parasites and treat as necessary. See pages 72 through 91.

Examine ears. See page 48.

Clean teeth if your dog's teeth demand it. See page 51.

Every two weeks: Check toenail length and appearance and trim, if necessary. See page 49.

Examine teeth if weekly cleaning is not necessary. See page 23.

Monthly: Examine mammary glands. See page 15.

Bathe, if necessary. See page 45.

Every six months: Perform a complete physical examination if one has not been indicated earlier.

Take a fecal sample to a veterinarian, particularly if there is an internal parasite problem in your area. See page 74.

Yearly: Take your dog to a veterinarian for a physical examination and booster vaccinations as necessary. See page 65.

Preventive Medicine

Preventive medicine is the best kind of medicine. Veterinarians practice it when they vaccinate your dog for certain communicable diseases (see page 65). You practice it by giving your dog good regular care at home as discussed in this section. If you practice preventive medicine, the occasions when your dog will need the care of a veterinarian can often be limited to yearly physical examinations and booster vaccinations. In the long run, preventive medicine will save you money and result in fewer stresses on your dog's body.

Training

Unless you want to mold your life around your dog's, you need to train them. I've seen dogs who only occasionally let their owners pick them up without attempting (often successfully) to bite. Many other dogs will not let their owners medicate or bathe them when necessary. These are examples of unhealthy dog-people relationships which I think can be avoided by acquiring some basic knowledge of dog behavior and obedience training. Since only a small part of this book is devoted to understanding your dog's behavior, and modifying it when necessary, you may find the following books useful:

Fox, M.W., *Understanding Your Dog;* Coward, McCann & Geoghegan, Inc., New York, 1972.

Fox, M.W., *Behavior of Wolves, Dogs and Related Canids,* Harper and Row, New York, 1971.

Scott, J.P. and Fuller, J.L., *Genetics and Social Behavior of the Dog,* University of Chicago Press, Chicago, 1965.

Lorenz, K., *Man Meets Dog,* Methuen, London, 1954.

Whitney, Leon F., *Dog Psychology, The Basis of Training,* 2nd ed., Howell Book House, New York, 1971.

Age to Get A Puppy

If you have a choice, the optimum time to bring home a new puppy is between six to eight weeks of age. This is a dog's optimum period for socialization to people. If a puppy is placed in an environment where there are no other dogs before six weeks of age, they may not become properly socialized to dogs. This can result in excessive fear of, or aggression towards, other dogs later in life, abnormal sexual behavior (e.g., inability to breed), or other dog-related behavioral problems. If the dog does not have close contact with people before eight to twelve weeks of age, they may never form a close human bond. Such dogs are often difficult to train and are often the type people find unsatisfying as companions. Of course there are exceptions to these generalities, but if you have a choice, you might as well start out with the best balance possible.

Punishment

Once you have your dog, you may more easily establish and maintain a good relationship if you remember that a domestic dog's behavior parallels that of wild pack canids, such as wolves, in many ways. Both form dominant-subordinate relationships easily. The dominant dog in a group (wolf in a pack) metes out fair punishment as necessary to maintain their position and the cohesiveness of the group. If you don't assert yourself as the dominant member of your dog-human "pack," your dog will.

In most cases *physical punishment is necessary to maintain your position only until your dog learns the meaning of the word, "No."* Once learned, this word is usually sufficient correction alone. To teach your dog the meaning of "No!," voice the command firmly in a *serious* tone of voice each time you show them that certain behavior is unacceptable. Punishment can consist of picking your dog up by the scruff and shaking them or holding their head or muzzle and pushing it to the ground. These methods mimic dominant be- havior in some wild canids. Although not as good as corrective measures, a rolled **PICKING UP BY SCRUFF OF NECK** newspaper or the flat of your hand can be used to spank your dog on the rump. If you choose to use one of these methods, try to avoid letting your dog see the spank coming and do not strike your dog around the head since doing so causes many dogs to become hand shy.

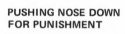

PUSHING NOSE DOWN FOR PUNISHMENT

A chain link training collar (choke collar) is also an acceptable method of correction. A sharp jerk on the collar is administered at the time the word "no" is spoken, then the collar is immediately loosened. If used properly, a choke collar is a humane and invaluable aid to obedience training. Used improperly, it is ineffective and can be very confusing to the dog. If you have never obedience-trained a dog before, I think it is best for you and your dog to attend dog obedience classes together. In such classes, your dog is exposed to other dogs and other people, and you are shown how to train your dog properly. In some areas there are no such classes available; you may have to resort to books for information on obedience training. The following should be helpful:

Obedience Training

Pearsall, N., *Successful Dog Training,* Howell Book House, Inc., New York, 1973.

Weatherwax, R. *The Lassie Method of Dog Training,* Western Publishing Co., 1971.

Saunders, B., *Training You to Train Your Dog,* Doubleday and Co., Garden City, New York, 1952.

41

Praise is extremely important to good training; it is your key to success. Praise must always follow punishment. As soon as your dog stops the behavior that calls for correction, tell them how good they are. And whenever your dog performs as expected, lavish praise upon them. If you make your dog feel like a success, they will be encouraged to behave in ways that please you and will enjoy doing it.

The establishment of a workable relationship between you and your dog should begin as soon as you bring them home. Training your dog to respond to simple commands such as "Sit!" and "Come" can begin as early as eight weeks of age if you are not too severe, avoid confusion, and if you limit the training session to short periods (five or ten minutes) two or three times a day. Formal obedience classes should be avoided until your dog finishes their vaccinations at four months of age.

If you don't want to share your bed with your dog, give them a place of their own the first night you have them home. An adult dog can be given an area indoors or, if used to being outside, a dog house in the yard or in a run. If your dog is a puppy, barricade a corner of a room or get a large box or traveling cage and place your dog's bed in it. Cover the remaining area with a layer of clean newspapers. Puppies should be kept indoors and gradually acclimatized to the outside. Unless they have been raised outdoors since birth, most can't adjust easily to the temperature stresses encountered outside.

At bedtime, take your dog outside to urinate and defecate, then place them in their bed area. After you assure yourself that your dog is warm and comfortable, leave them in this area. The first time you do this your dog will probably cry. When they do, tell them "No!" seriously and firmly, make them comfortable and, as soon as they are quiet, praise them and leave them alone. This series of events may have to be repeated several times, but there is a point where you may just have to ignore the crying. DON'T GIVE IN. Generally after a few minutes the dog will fall asleep. Even if your dog cries frequently the first couple of nights, the lack of sleep and emotional stress of hearing your dog cry is worth it in the long run. It is a good idea to leave your dog in their special area any time you have to leave them alone, and at other times when you are home but it is inconvenient to have the dog loose. If you are consistent, your dog will soon regard the area as their refuge or "den." This method is also useful to achieve early housebreaking.

Housebreaking consists of repeatedly showing your dog the proper place to eliminate, praising them when they use it, and punishing them when they don't. Domestic dogs, like their wild counterparts, do not like to soil their "dens." If at all possible, a puppy will not urinate or defecate in their bed. By restricting your dog's freedom at night and when you must leave them alone, you encourage them to retain urine and feces as long as possible. If they have to go, they will go on the newspapers making clean up much easier. The learning process is probably easier for your dog if you housebreak them directly to the outside using papers only as an emergency measure during the night. With time your dog will progress from regarding only their small area as a den to regarding your whole house as a den and will be inhibited from eliminating indoors. Rules that make housebreaking easier:

1. Take your puppy out when they awaken, not only first thing in the morning, but after naps as well.

2. DO NOT send your puppy out alone. Go with them and stay out until they eliminate so you can give praise for the right behavior.

3. Take them out about twenty minutes after eating. The *gastrocolic reflex* stimulates most dogs to defecate about this long after eating or playing.

4. Give your puppy their last meal early in the evening and take them out before bed. It is best to have water available at all times for your dog, but, while you are housebreaking them, water may be removed at night.

5. Punish your dog only when you catch them eliminating in the wrong place. If possible snatch them up in the middle of the act with a "No!," and get them to finish outdoors so you can them give praise. Punishment for elimination in the wrong place administered several hours after the act is not very effective.

Most dogs are not housebroken before about twelve weeks of age. No dog should be expected to remain continent for more than about eight hours (although many can), and

43

many dogs are unable to pass a full night without elimination until they are five to six months old. If you can provide your dog access to an enclosed yard through a "dog door," you may solve the housebreaking problem more quickly.

Puppies investigate their environment by sight, smell, hearing and CHEWING. It's reasonable to punish your dog for chewing on things that they're not supposed to, but unreasonable to expect them not to chew at all. Provide your dog with acceptable things to chew on — rawhide toys, large hard rubber toys — and praise them when they use their toys. Never give them objects which are easily torn into pieces or are small enough for them to swallow (even with difficulty). I have seen several rubber balls, pieces of carpeting, parts of a tennis shoe, and other objects removed from dogs' digestive tracts. One veterinarian at least has removed a large mechanical monkey from a relatively small dog's stomach, and a recent journal article described a dog which had swallowed a large carving knife whole! Avoid giving your dog objects such as old shoes or socks to chew on; they are too easily confused with possessions you don't want chewed.

Bones for chewing have their pros and cons. They satisfy a dog's chewing urge and help keep their teeth clean, but too much bone chewing can lead to excessively worn teeth. Bones which get eaten rather than just chewed on are a common cause of *gastritis* ("stomach ache," see page 131) and constipation. If you choose to give your dog bones, they should be large enough and hard enough that they can't be eaten. Marrow bones or knucklebones are usually the best choices unless your dog is very

KNUCKLE BONE   **MARROW BONE**

small. It is best to parboil these bones before allowing your dog to chew on them to avoid the transmission of some parasites. Don't give poultry bones, pork chop bones, steak bones or other bones that can be splintered. If you see that your dog is *eating* a bone, take it away. More than one dog has died from a gut perforation caused by a sharp bone splinter.

44

Although dogs resemble wild canids in many ways, keep it in mind that they are *domesticated* animals with very different needs than those of their wild counterparts. One of the outstanding characteristics of most dogs, particularly when they are young, is their adaptability. Some dogs have a greater need for activity than others, but no dog has an innate need to run free. If you let your dog run free while they are young they will adapt to and expect this condition, but, if you restrict their roaming, they will adapt as readily to this situation. Most dogs' needs for activity can be met by taking them for short walks two or three times a day, through goal-directed play periods such as ball chasing, obedience lessons, or by giving them free access to an enclosed yard with a companion — you, another dog or a cat. City dogs should not be allowed to run the streets unsupervised. Not only do most cities have laws prohibiting this, but roaming city dogs are among those I see injured or ill most often. They are exposed to communicable diseases as they make their territorial rounds; they are hit by cars; they are poisoned; they get in dog fights much more often than dogs accompanied by their owners. I think you are doing a city dog a great disservice if you allow them to roam. If you live in a rural area away from automobile traffic, it may be safe to let your dog loose. However, if you live where there is livestock, be careful. Many dogs have been shot, both justly and unjustly, by disgruntled livestock owners. In other cases they have been poisoned by bait left out for wild predators.

Grooming

Regular grooming makes a dog nicer to live with and to look at, and is usually responsible for making them feel more comfortable. It is important, as well, in maintaining a healthy coat and skin.

Bathing

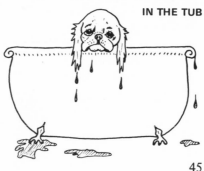

IN THE TUB

How often you bathe your dog depends not only on how frequently they get dirty, but on the type of skin and hair they have, and the kind of cleanser you use. The average

Skin pH normal dog is said to maintain a slightly alkaline skin pH, as opposed to the acid environment of human skin. Actually, healthy dogs have a range of skin pH, and shampoos designed for dogs, like human shampoos, vary from acid to alkaline depending on the product. Unless your dog has a specific skin

Shampoo problem requiring medicated shampoo recommended by a *to Use* veterinarian, use a good quality dog shampoo or gentle human shampoo (e.g., baby shampoo) for bathing. Avoid bar soap and dishwashing detergents since they seem to be particularly drying or irritating to some dogs' skin and hair.

How Often If you use a good quality shampoo, most dogs can be *to Bathe* bathed about once a month. Some dogs need to be bathed much more frequently; others should be bathed less frequently. Use your dog's appearance, feel and odor as guides.

When to Accustom your dog to bathing early in life so it won't *Start Baths* be a problem later. You can bathe a puppy as young as seven or eight weeks of age if you do it quickly and prevent chilling. Bathing itself does not cause illness, but the stress of being chilled can predispose any dog, particularly a young one, to disease.

How to It is usually easiest for you and most comfortable for *Bathe* your dog if you use a sink or bathtub and warm water for bathing. If the weather is warm, however, bathing can be done outside using water from a garden hose. This method is usually the easiest for very large dogs. Before the bath it is a good idea, but not absolutely necessary, to protect your dog's ear canals and eyes from the soap and water. This can be done by placing large wads of cotton firmly inside the ears and by applying a gentle ophthalmic ointment, petrolatum or a drop of mineral oil into each eye. Long-haired dogs should be combed out before bathing so grooming after the bath is easier.

If you accustom your dog to bathing at a young age you should have no difficulty during baths. Adult dogs who have never been bathed or allowed to swim when young may never adjust well to baths, however. If your dog seems very insecure in the tub, a rubber mat placed in the bottom of the bathtub will provide some traction and perhaps relieve some fears. A soft rope looped around the neck and tied to a fixture (*never* a hot water faucet) will keep most

46

uncooperative dogs in the tub. But never leave a dog tied in this manner alone. Use the basic rules of training to get your dog to cooperate. "No" when they try to get out of the tub. Praise when they stand quietly. As a last resort, your veterinarian can provide tranquilizers to use when bathing an extremely unmanageable dog.

Start the bath by wetting your dog thoroughly, then apply the shampoo and suds it up. Two shampoo applications may be necessary if your dog is very dirty. Thorough rinsing is extremely important since any soap left on the skin can be very irritating. A human or dog creme rinse, used according to directions after the shampoo, makes the combout of long-haired dogs easier. Towel drying is usually sufficient, but if you accustom your dog to the sound, you can use a human hair drier to speed the process. Be sure to prevent your dog from becoming chilled while drying.

Grooming Between Baths

The kind of grooming your dog's coat needs between baths depends on its length and character. Short-haired dogs usually need only an occasional rubdown with a hound mitt to remove loose hair and distribute the oils. Dogs with longer

GROOMING AIDS

Wire Comb

Card Brush

Bristle Brush

Grooming Mitt

Rake

hair need more specialized grooming. In addition to regular combing and brushing, many breeds need periodic clipping and/or plucking to keep their coats in manageable condition

Hair Mats and the hair out of their eyes. Mats of hair often occur behind the ears and under the legs. These can be teased apart with a comb when they are small. If allowed to become large, such mats must be cut away with scissors or clippers.

Foxtails In areas such as California where *foxtails* (wild barley) or other troublesome plant awns (seeds) grow, longer-haired dogs need to have their coats examined for awns daily in the late spring, summer and fall. Particular attention should be paid to the areas between the toes, under the legs, and around the ears and genitals. Awns not discovered

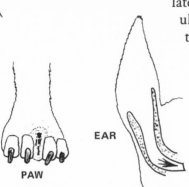

PAW

EAR

VULVA

and removed easily penetrate the skin, travel down the ear canals or up the genital tract causing irritation and infection.

Skunk odor If your dog gets sprayed by a skunk, bathe them in soap and water then follow with a tomato juice soak. Pour on the juice straight; let it sit for about ten minutes, then rinse it out. If you don't have access to tomato juice you can follow the bath with a dilute rinse of ammonia. If you rinse with ammonia, be sure to keep it out of your dog's eyes.

Tar, paint Tar and paint are difficult substances to remove from the coat. DO NOT use gasoline, turpentine, kerosene, paint remover or other similar substances in an attempt to remove them. Cut out small accumulations of tar or paint. Large amounts of tar can be removed without cutting by soaking in vegetable or mineral oil for twenty-four hours (e.g., bandage feet soaked in oil), then washing with soap and water.

Ears

General Most dogs need to have their ears cleaned about once a
Ear Care month. It is easy to do after bathing using a damp towel or soft cloth. Wrap the cloth over your index finger, then clean

48

out the excess wax and dirt that has accumulated in the pinna and as far down the ear canal as your finger will reach. You cannot damage the ear drum in this way. Any folds or crevices you cannot reach into with your finger can be cleaned using a cotton-tipped swab moistened with water, mineral oil or isopropyl alcohol. If your dog has an inflammation or infection of the ear *(otitis)* special ear cleaning may be necessary (see page 174).

Some veterinarians feel that ear canals that have hair in them should have the hair removed periodically to prevent ear inflammations. Dogs such as poodles and poodle-crosses, terriers and terrier-crosses usually have hairy ear canals.

Hairy Ear Canals

If your dog's ears have so much hair in them that the ear canals are blocked, so air can't circulate, if large amounts of wax accumulate, or if there is irritation of the canals, pluck the hair from them. Otherwise, plucking is probably not necessary.

To pluck ear canal hair, grasp protruding hair with your fingers or a pair of tweezers and give a quick jerk. Hair in the ear canal usually comes out easily, and the plucking process does not seem to be painful if done properly and if the ear canal is not inflamed. Be careful not to tug on the hair just outside the ear canal — this hurts. Hair not easily removed by plucking will need to be clipped out.

Toenails

Dogs' toenails should be no longer than the length it takes for them to just touch the ground, allowing the foot to remain compact and trim. Longer nails do not provide good traction and cause a dog to stand abnormally, sometimes causing pain. Sometimes toenails will grow in a complete circle penetrating the pad. This is a particular problem with dewclaws which do not touch the ground as they grow out.

Proper Toenail Length

49

Not all dogs need their nails trimmed. Large dogs that exercise outdoors a great deal usually keep their nails worn down to the proper length. Small dogs and dogs that spend most of their time indoors usually do need their nails cut, however. Dogs with long hair on their feet are often allowed to grow nails to excessive lengths. If you have a long-haired dog, be sure to check the toenail length frequently.

How to Trim Toenails
Light-colored nails are easiest to trim since the dermis (quick) can be seen when the nail is held up to the light. Cut the nail just beyond the point where you see the dermis end. If you cut into the dermis, it is painful and some bleeding will usually occur. The bleeding stops, but the pain will make your dog reluctant to have a nail trim the next time. Black

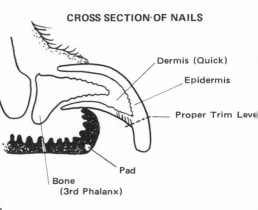

CROSS SECTION OF NAILS

Dermis (Quick)

Epidermis

Proper Trim Level

Pad

Bone (3rd Phalanx)

nails are harder to trim. The easiest rule to follow is to cut the nail just beyond the point where it starts to curve downward.

The dermis seems to get longer in nails which have been allowed to grow too long. Sometimes it can be driven back and the nails shortened to their proper length by frequent filing or running on a hard surface. The only other alternative is to have the nails trimmed short under anesthesia, then keep them the proper length.

"RESCO" NAIL TRIMMER

"WHITE" NAIL TRIMMER

There are two common types of nail clippers, White's and Resco's. I find the White's type the most manuverable, and they are my preference for all except large dogs. If you trim a nail into the quick and the bleeding doesn't seem to be stopping,

50

you can apply a styptic pencil to the area or bandage the foot firmly for about an hour (see p. 176). One of these methods usually works to stop the bleeding.

Teeth

Almost all dogs, particularly small breeds, need special attention given to their teeth to preserve them and to minimize mouth odors. Most dogs, like most people, develop *Tartar* deposits called dental *tartar* or *calculus* on their teeth. When present it is most obvious on the canine teeth and molars as a hard yellow-brown or grayish-white deposit which cannot be removed by brushing or scraping with a fingernail. Its presence is *not* normal (see page 23). It causes gum disease which can eventually lead to loss of teeth. *Periodontal* (gum) disease is the most frequently seen mouth disease in dogs. Most do not develop cavities, but lose teeth because their owners miss the early stages of gum disease.

Once tartar is present it can only be removed properly *Tartar* with special instruments — tartar scrapers or an ultra-sonic *Prevention* tooth cleaner. Tartar is best removed by a veterinarian or dentist (if you can find one interested in cleaning your dog's teeth). Tartar originates from a soft white to yellow-colored substance called *materia alba* or plaque. You can remove this and prevent tartar formation in the following ways:

1. Feed your dog dry food. Dogs which eat a kibble or biscuit diet tend to have less tartar, possibly due to the abrasive action of this type of food. Feeding a hard food diet will not absolutely prevent tartar in all dogs because its formation is dependent on conditions in each dog's mouth, not only on their diet. Some dogs, particularly small breeds, seem to form lots of plaque and tartar no matter what diet is fed.

2. Give your dog things to chew on — hard rubber toys, rawhide toys, bones big enough and hard enough to prevent swallowing them. These toys remove plaque by abrasion.

3. Clean your dog's teeth yourself once or twice a week. You can use a toothbrush and toothpaste, but a gauze pad found in drugstores or a rough cloth works as well. Moisten it with water, water and salt, or water and sodium bicarbonate, then scrub the teeth and gums vigorously. It's not absolutely necessary to do the inner tooth surfaces,

CLEANING THE TEETH

because the motion of the tongue usually keeps the areas next to it relatively free of plaque.

If your dog's gums bleed even though they look healthy otherwise, it is not usually because you have scrubbed too hard but because they are in the early stages of disease. Good tooth care should cause an early problem to correct itself. If you see that the gums are red, and pulling away from the teeth (receding), you probably will need the help of a veterinarian to clear up the condition. Loose teeth will have to be removed and dirty ones cleaned. You can begin treatment at home with daily gum massage. Use your finger bare or wrapped in a cloth. Make gentle motions while pressing gently, but firmly, against the gums and teeth.

RECEDING GUMS

Nutrition

Most dog owners will face three distinct feeding situations: feeding the puppy; feeding the adult dog; feeding the old dog. The formulation of a diet to satisfy a dog's needs during each of these periods in life, and at times of special nutrient requirements, is difficult, time consuming and a practice most dog owners seem not to be interested in. If you think you would like to feed your dog from scratch, use a proven receipe such as those included here or which your veterinarian may be able to supply. Or begin your reading with the following before trying to formulate a diet yourself:

General Feeding Information

Foo-Foo

National Research Council, *Nutrient Requirements of Dogs,* National Academy of Sciences, Washington, D.C., 1974.

Collins, D.R., *The Collins Guide to Dog Nutrition,* Howell Book House, Inc., New York, 1973. (Excellent supplement to this section and much more detailed. Tells you how to formulate your own home diet.)

Dogs meet their nutritional requirements by ingesting proteins, carbohydrates, fats, vitamins and minerals just as humans do. Minimum requirements of each kind of nutrient, except carbohydrates, have been established for dogs (see tables pages 55 and 56) and *reputable* dog food manufacturers formulate the *rations* (complete daily diets) they sell to meet these established requirements. *In general,* commercial dry or soft-moist foods are more reliably balanced products than canned rations available in grocery stores.

Proteins are essential for growth and repair. They *Proteins* cannot be synthesized in the body from dietary constituents other than protein. Therefore they are extremely important to nutrition. Proteins are composed of amino acids and vary widely in their kinds and proportions.

Home Diet For Dogs I*

½ cup farina (commonly known as Cream of Wheat®), cooked to make 2 cups
1 cup creamed cottage cheese
1 large whole egg, hard cooked
2 tablespoons dry active baker's yeast
3 tablespoons granulated sugar or 1 tablespoon honey
1 tablespoon corn oil or lard

Cook farina according to package directions. Cool. Add remaining ingredients and mix well. This recipe yields about 1¾ pounds food containing approximately 425 calories per pound.

For growing dogs add to the above:

2 large whole eggs, hard cooked
or
2 ounces canned mackerel
or
1¾ ounce cooked ground beef or lamb, or liver

Home Diet For Dogs II*

Cook as a stew:

1 pound ground beef
1 large can stewed tomatoes
6 large potatoes
2 large onions
1 cup macaroni
1 pound dry rice
2 cups water
juice of 2 cans yellow beans
juice of 2 cans green beans
juice of 2 cans carrots

Add green beans, yellow beans, and carrots, and mix well. This makes ten quarts of food to be fed at the rate of about one quart per forty pounds body weight per day. (This is a restricted protein diet and, as such, may not be suitable for growing puppies.)

These diets could be mixed with a commercial balanced dry diet to provide a feeding method half way between "homecooking" and "store bought."

*My thanks to Dr. Mark Morris of Mark Morris Associates, Topeka, Kansas for supplying the basic recipes for these diets.

Nutrient Requirements of Dogs
Amount (percentage) needed per kilogram food*

		Type of Diet			
		Dry Basis	Dry Type	Semi-moist	Canned or Wet
Moisture level (%):		0	10	25	75
Dry-matter basis (%):		100	90	75	25
Nutrient		**Requirement**			
Protein	%	22	20	16.5	5.5
Fat	%	5.5	5.0	4	2
Linoleic or arachidonic acid	%	1.6	1.4	1.2	0.4
Carbohydrate	%	67.0	60.0	50.0	17.0
Minerals					
Calcium	%	1.1	1.0	0.8	0.3
Phosphorus	%	0.9	0.8	0.7	0.25
Potassium	%	0.6	0.5	0.45	0.2
Sodium chloride	%	1.0	0.9	0.8	0.3
Magnesium	%	0.05	0.04	0.03	0.01
Iron	mg	57.32	51.59	42.99	14.33
Copper	mg	7.28	6.55	5.47	1.83
Cobalt	mg	2.43	2.18	1.83	0.62
Manganese	mg	4.85	4.37	3.64	1.21
Zinc	mg	110	99.21	82.67	27.56
Iodine	mg	1.54	1.39	1.17	0.40
Vitamins					
Vitamin A	mg	1.5[a]	1.4	1.2	0.4
Vitamin D	mg	0.012[b]	0.006	0.005	0.002
Vitamin E	mg	48.5	43.65	36.38	12.13
Vitamin B_{12}	mg	0.02	0.02	0.015	0.005
Folic acid	mg	0.18	0.17	0.13	0.04
Thiamine	mg	0.97	0.87	0.73	0.24
Riboflavin	mg	2.16	1.94	1.63	0.55
Pyridoxine	mg	0.97	0.88	0.73	0.24
Pantothenic acid	mg	2.18	1.96	1.63	0.55
Niacin	mg	10.58	9.52	7.94	2.65
Choline	mg	1,200	1,100	900	300
Vitamin K	mg	1.4	1.3	1.1	0.4

[a] This amount of crystalline A corresponds to 5,000 IU per kg of feed.

[b] This amount of pure vitamin D corresponds to 484 IU per kg of feed.

Nutrient Requirements of Dogs
Amount needed per kilogram body weight per day*

Nutrient		Adult Maintenance	Growing Puppies
Protein	g	4.4	8.8
Fat	g	1.3	2.6
Linoleic or			
Arachidonic acid	g	0.4	0.7
Carbohydrate	g	15.4	30.8
Minerals			
Calcium	mg	253	506
Phosphorus	mg	207	414
Potassium	mg	138	276
Sodium chloride	mg	230	460
Magnesium	mg	11.5	23
Iron	mg	1.30	2.6
Copper	mg	0.17	0.334
Cobalt	mg	0.055	0.112
Manganese	mg	0.110	0.22
Zinc	mg	2.5	5.1
Iodine	mg	0.035	0.070
Vitamins			
Vitamin A	IU	115	230
Vitamin D	IU	11	22.0
Vitamin E			
(alpha tocopherol)	mg	1.1	2.2
Vitamin B_{12}	μg	0.46	0.92
Folic acid	μg	4.1	8.3
Thiamine	μg	22.3	44.6
Riboflavin	μg	49.7	99.4
Pyridoxine	μg	22.3	44.6
Pantothenic acid	μg	50.1	100.3
Niacin	μg	243	487
Choline	mg	27.9	55.8
Vitamin K	μg	32.2	64.4

DEFINITIONS:
g = gram, approximately 1/30 ounce
kg = kilogram, one thousand grams, approximately 2.2 pounds
mg = milligram, 1/1000 gram
μg = microgram, 1/1,000,000 gram
IU = international unit, a measure of vitamin activity. The amount in
      milligrams varies depending on the vitamin under consideration.

*Nutrient Requirements of Dogs, Publication ISBN 0-309-02043-3, Committee on Animal Nutrition, National Academy of Sciences – National Research Council, Washington, D.C., 1974.

Essential amino acids cannot be synthesized in the dog's body and must be supplied by the diet in special proportions for optimum use. Proteins which supply the essential amino acids in nearly optimum quantities are given a high *biological value* because they are utilized efficiently by the body. Proteins with high biological value are the best ones to feed. Examples of such proteins are eggs, muscle meat, milk, fish meal, soybeans, and yeast. Protein deficiencies usually occur when dogs are fed diets based on high carbohydrate, low biological value plant substances or which use poor quality animal protein (e.g., tankage) deficient in essential amino acids as a protein source in a mainly cereal diet.

Eggs are an excellent source of protein of high biological value, but, if fed frequently, should be cooked. Egg white is not digested as well raw as when cooked. It also contains a substance called *avidin* which binds *biotin* (an important B vitamin) preventing its absorption from the gut.

Milk, and milk products such as cottage cheese or yogurt, are also good sources of protein as well as of calcium and phosphorus. Some dogs develop diarrhea when fed any milk products; others may develop diarrhea only when fed large amounts of them. Diarrhea associated with the ingestion of milk products occurs when *lactose* (milk sugar) is not digested. Undigested lactose attracts water into the intestine, causing diarrhea. For this reason it is often recommended that a dog's diet contain no more than 20% milk. Dogs that cannot drink milk without developing diarrhea can often eat yogurt — which has a much lower lactose content.

Carbohydrates

Carbohydrates (cellulose, starch, sugars) are used by the dog as energy sources and, under normal metabolic conditions, to maintain the blood glucose level. Because carbohydrates are readily available as energy sources, they "spare" proteins allowing them to be used for more important structural uses in the body instead. Cellulose, an indigestible carbohydrate in the dog, provides necessary bulk for normal intestinal function.

Although a minimum level of carbohydrate requirement has not been established for dogs, they readily digest large amounts of carbohydrate, (e.g., cereal grains, potatoes) particularly when cooked. And since carbohydrates are inexpensive nutrient sources, they are widely used as a basis

57

for commercial dog diets. Authorities recommend that no more than 50% to 65% of a dog's diet (on a dry weight basis) be composed of carbohydrates, in order to allow for sufficient protein, fat and minerals in the diet.

Fats　　Fats provide the most concentrated source of energy (nine Calories per gram) of any of the necessary dietary components. They carry fat soluble vitamins (D,E,A,K) and supply the essential fatty acid, linoleic acid, important for healthy skin and hair. The fat requirement varies depending on the individual fat's degree of saturation and its essential fatty acid content. Linoleic acid should supply 2% or more of the energy of the diet (0.7% to 2.1% weight of a dried ration). This quantity is usually found in commercial dry food containing 5% to 8% by weight of fat.

Fat's Effect on　　A deficiency of essential fatty acid can retard puppies'
"Dry" Skin　growth and produce coarse hair and dry, flaking skin. The idea that a young (or old) dog with scaly skin needs more dietary fat, however, is probably overworked, since most commercial diets provide sufficient levels of unsaturated fatty acids. Scaly skin and dry coat can also be caused by distinct disease processes not related to diet, and good skin health is dependent on an interaction of various nutrients as well as on fatty acid.

If you think your dog has a fatty acid deficiency you can supplement the diet with one to one and one-half tablespoonsful per pound dry food of lard, bacon fat or vegetable oil (safflower, corn, soybean, or cotton seed oil are good). Canned foods containing 2% to 3.5% fat (on an as fed basis) can have fat added at about one tablespoon per one pound can. Soft-moist foods or canned foods containing more than 6% fat should not have fat added. By increasing the fat content of the diet so that it supplies more than 40% of the daily caloric requirement total food consumption can be lowered enough to induce other nutritional deficiencies, so beware. Skin improvement is usually seen one to two months after beginning supplementation if fat content is causing the problem. A better approach to treating unhealthy skin resulting from dietary deficiencies may be to use a balanced nutritional supplement containing polyunsaturated fatty acids, vitamins A and E, pyridoxine and zinc. Or discuss the problem with your veterinarian.

Dogs require about twenty-five milliliters (¾ oz.) water per pound of body weight daily. They obtain this water in the food they eat and the liquids they drink. Water is also a by-product of metabolism. A dog can go without food for days and lose 30% to 40% of its normal body weight without dying, but a water loss of 10% to 15% can be fatal. The actual amount of liquid a dog must drink daily is influenced by many factors (among them diet, exercise, environmental temperature, presence of vomiting or diarrhea). So the best solution to the problem of water intake is to be sure that your dog has access to clean water at all times. Do not give them water considered unfit for human consumption. If you are unable to give your dog free water access, offer water at least three times a day.

A study of the interrelationships between the minerals *Calcium,* calcium and phosphorus and the vitamin D emphasize the *Phosphorus,* importance of feeding a balanced diet and the importance of *Vitamin D* *not* using unnecessary dietary supplements in the form of unbalanced vitamin and mineral preparations.

Calcium and phosphorus should be present in the diet as a ratio of about 1.2 to 1. If an adequate amount of each of these minerals is present, but the ratio is incorrect, abnormal mineralization of bone occurs in the growing puppy as well as in the adult dog. If adequate amounts of calcium and phosphorus in the proper ratio are provided, but without sufficient vitamin D, abnormalities of bone result again. Insufficient levels of vitamin D interfere with calcium absorption from the gut. Excessive amounts of vitamin D in the presence of adequate levels of calcium and phosphorus may result in excessive mineralization of bone, abnormal teeth, hypertension and calcification of the soft tissues of the body. The delicacy of these relationships is apparent.

The calcium:phosphorus ratio found in raw beef, beef *Say "No!" to All* liver and horsemeat is about 1 to 15. This fact alone, I think, *Meat Diets* makes it fairly obvious that feeding your dog an all meat diet is not doing them any favors. In addition, the amount of raw beef sufficient to meet the caloric requirements of a twenty pound dog supplies inadequate amounts of the vitamins D, A and E; inadequate iron, sodium, potassium, cobalt, copper, magnesium and iodine; and an excessive amount of fat. All meat diets are also noted for their ability to produce diarrhea and flatulence in many dogs. They may also place an excessive metabolic load on an older dog with failing kidneys. Feed your dog a balanced canned, soft-moist or dry food as a basic diet. All meat products and other high protein foods can be used as a supplement and to improve flavor, if you use them at no more than about 25% of the total diet. (One pound meat to one pound dry food or one pound meat to nine cans wet complete diet. One cooked egg per three pounds dry dog food or one can wet complete diet.)

Avoid Diet Supplements Many dog breeders and many owners of large breeds of dogs have become believers in a practice that can easily do more harm to than good for their dogs — routine supplementation of the diet with *unbalanced* vitamin and/or mineral substances (e.g., bone meal alone, cod liver oil). Unbalanced supplements can result in abnormalities of structure and function every bit as severe as those you are trying to prevent. (For example vitamin D excess causes hypertension and secondary kidney damage.) At best excess nutrients such as calcium and phosphorus will be excreted unused.

Cod Liver Oil Cod liver oil should not be used as a routine daily supplement for dogs. One-half teaspoon of N.F. cod liver oil (312 IU per teaspoon) provides more than the required vitamin D per pound dry diet. Regular use, particularly with an already balanced diet, can lead to vitamin D excess.

The best procedure is to feed only a balanced diet. If you feel that you must use supplementation to assure yourself that your dog is getting all the vitamins and minerals needed, use a *balanced* vitamin-mineral supplement which provides the substances in the proper proportions and follow your veterinarian's or the manufacturers directions carefully to supply only the minimum daily requirement for each nutrient.

Choosing A Dog Food Federal law requires that all dog foods carry a listing of ingredients in decreasing order of predominance in the ration. Other regulations require a guaranteed analysis listing minimum or maximum levels of certain nutrients present. Unfortunately, the required labels do not contain enough information to enable you to compare dog foods adequately with one another. The guaranteed analysis gives no indication of the *quality* of the nutrients present nor does it give the exact quantities present. Companies are restricted from misrepresenting their products, however, and certain large manufacturers of dog foods have conducted extensive research and feeding trials in order to produce nutritious diets that need no supplementation. The following rules of thumb will help you choose a dog food:

1. Look at the food. This is a fairly effective way of evaluating many canned foods. If you see pieces of bone, discolored meat and poorly digestible items such as blood vessels and skin, it's a pretty good indicator of poor quality.

2. Consider the price. Cheap dog foods often contain cheap ingredients — poor quality protein and poorly digestible nutrients which pass through your dog unused. "Gourmet" type dog foods, on the other hand, may contain high quality ingredients but are often overpriced as well.

3. Well-known manufacturers noted for their research generally produce good quality dog foods you can trust.

4. See what kind of effect the food has when eaten. If your dog gets diarrhea or becomes flatulent on a food, it's not the diet you should continue to feed. Voluminous stools following feeding of certain brands of food often indicate excessive amounts of fiber or other undigestible substances.

5. Write the dog food manufacturer for a complete analysis of the dog food you would like to use and compare it with the tables on pages 55 and 56.

Feeding a Puppy

Dogs under eight months of age require about twice as much protein and about 50% more calories per pound body weight daily than adult dogs. These special needs can be most easily filled by feeding a diet based on a good quality commercial puppy chow. Adult dog food can be used, but the protein content must be increased by adding a good quality supplement such as milk, eggs, or meat.

Changing a Puppy's Diet

If your puppy has not already been started on a commercial diet when you take them home, find out what has been fed and continue feeding this diet for a few days, gradually switching over to a complete ration. Rapid changes in diet often cause gastrointestinal upsets in young dogs, characterized by diarrhea.

How Often To Feed

Self-feeding is the most convenient method for a young dog. In this method the food is left out where the dog has

61

free access to it and is changed as necessary to keep it fresh. Most puppies will not overeat with this system and it seems to prevent boredom in dogs who must be left alone. If the self-feeding method is not suitable, feed your puppy four times a day until about three months old, three times a day until about six months old, then twice daily until fully grown. A combination of self-feeding and scheduled feeding can be used as well.

How Much To Feed As a rough guide, puppies need about one hundred Calories per pound of body weight per day. Information on the dog food package can also be used as a feeding guide. But remember that each dog is an individual and has individualized caloric requirements. If you are feeding a balanced diet, your best guide is your dog's appearance. Look at and feel your puppy. If the spine and ribs are prominent, you may not be feeding enough. Each meal should comfortably fill a puppy. If your dog's stomach is distended and taut following a meal, or if they vomit shortly after eating, they may be eating too much at one time. More frequent, smaller meals may be necessary.

Table scraps Most dogs will prefer canned meat or table scraps to a commercial dry or semi-moist dog food. However, don't let this lead you into feeding your puppy an unbalanced diet. If you don't routinely feed large quantities of meat or other "goodies," they won't be demanded. If you feel that the commercial food needs a flavor supplement, add chicken or beef broth, or canned meat, milk or eggs — at not more than 25% of the diet. Use tablescraps carefully; feed them only as a special treat and avoid fatty or spicy foods that can upset your dog's digestion.

Feeding an Adult Dog

As your puppy becomes an adult, you can switch from a puppy ration to an adult dog food, or decrease the protein supplements if you have been using an adult ration as a basic diet. Self-feeding can be continued, but if you notice your dog becoming overweight, you will have to switch to one or two individual meals per day. Some dogs vomit clear or yellow-tinged stomach juices if fed only once every twenty-four hours. These dogs benefit by being fed two smaller meals (breakfast and dinner) daily.

Although most adult dogs require about forty Calories per pound body weight per day, as with puppies each individual has individual requirements. During cold weather dogs kenneled outside need more Calories. Working dogs require more Calories than sedentary ones. Pregnant and lactating females also have special requirements (see pages 198 and 204), and with some illnesses your veterinarian will suggest special diets.

Feeding an Old Dog

Dogs undergo aging changes just like humans do and often require special diets for maximum health and activity in old age. In general, older dogs require fewer Calories per pound body weight than when they were young; the amount of food given must usually be decreased in order to avoid obesity. Body changes can result in decreased utilization of nutrients; additionally, intestinal absorption of nutrients may be impaired. There is then a rationale for using balanced vitamin-mineral preparations to supplement the older dog's diet. Dietary fat should be kept at the minimum level necessary to fulfill essential fatty acid requirements since some older dogs seem to have greater difficulty digesting fats and since the Calories excess fat provides increase the likelihood of obesity. Certain diseases such as heart or kidney failure which tend to occur more often in old dogs (see pages 163 and 164) require special diets. The presence of such conditions should be determined by a veterinarian, however, before any special diet is used.

Prevent Trichinosis

Trichinosis is a roundworm infection disseminated primarily in pork. It occurs when the larval forms of *Trichinella spiralis*, which encyst in muscle tissue, are eaten. This disease affects humans, pigs, and other mammals including dogs and rats. The infection can cause severe muscular pain. Prevent trichinosis by not feeding raw or undercooked pork to your dog. You may want to avoid giving your dog any pork at all since some dogs get indigestion after eating it.

Traveling With or Shipping a Dog

Sooner or later most dog owners have to make a decision about traveling with their dog. If you accustom your dog to riding in automobiles and to confinement when they are young, many travel problems are avoided. Take your dog for frequent short rides at first, then gradually lengthen them. And remember to enforce good behavior from the start. An adult dog that does not sit or lie quietly while traveling can be very annoying and sometimes very dangerous. See page 132 for information on motion sickness, and see page 158 for information on heat stress which often occurs when dogs are confined improperly while traveling.

The following items may help you when traveling with or shipping your dog on commercial carriers:

1. Most states require evidence of current rabies vaccination and a health certificate signed by an accredited veterinarian for entry. Airlines require these documents for shipping. Each foreign country has its own entry requirements for animals. Veterinarians can usually supply information regarding U.S. requirements; individual consulates are the best sources of current information for each foreign country.

2. Your veterinarian can prescribe safe tranquilizers for your dog if they are apprehensive about strange people and sounds. I think these are helpful for the average dog traveling in a baggage compartment. Seasoned travelers may not need them, however, and their use in dogs with special problems, such as bulldogs, may not be recommended by your veterinarian. If your dog is small, special arrangements may be made for them to travel with you in the passenger area.

3. A traveling crate should be strong and have enough room to enable your dog to stand up, turn around, and lie down comfortably.

4. Attach an identification tag to *both* the crate and the dog stating the owner's name, dog's name, address, and destination.

5. Exercise your dog before shipping.

6. Do not feed within eight hours prior to shipping.

7. Avoid giving water within about two hours of shipping unless absolutely necessary (such as conditions of extreme heat).

8. Do not place food or water in the crate. A *healthy* dog can go twenty-four hours without water, unless the environmental temperature is high, and much longer without food. If the trip is going to take longer than twenty-four hours, be *sure* special arrangements are made for feeding, watering, and exercise.

Preventive Vaccination Procedures

There are four major infectious canine diseases for which safe and effective vaccines are available: rabies, canine distemper, hepatitis and leptospirosis. Each of these diseases easily causes death in an unprotected dog. We are very fortunate to be able to prevent such serious illnesses with a procedure as technically simple as vaccination.

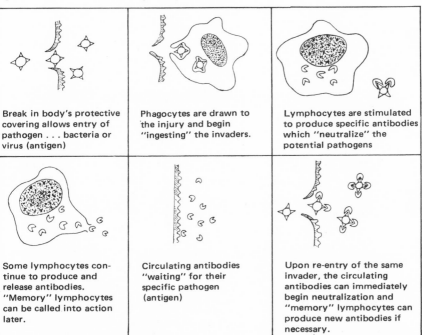

| Break in body's protective covering allows entry of pathogen . . . bacteria or virus (antigen) | Phagocytes are drawn to the injury and begin "ingesting" the invaders. | Lymphocytes are stimulated to produce specific antibodies which "neutralize" the potential pathogens |
| Some lymphocytes continue to produce and release antibodies. "Memory" lymphocytes can be called into action later. | Circulating antibodies "waiting" for their specific pathogen (antigen) | Upon re-entry of the same invader, the circulating antibodies can immediately begin neutralization and "memory" lymphocytes can produce new antibodies if necessary. |

How Vaccines Work

Antigens are molecules that have particular areas on their surfaces which are recognized as foreign to the body. *Antibodies* are protein substances produced in the body which are responsible for recognizing these antigens. They are

How Vaccines Work

65

produced by cells called *lymphocytes* which originate in the bone marrow and multiply in the thymus, spleen and lymph nodes. When lymphocytes recognize that a foreign substance (antigen) such as a virus or bacterium has entered the body, they begin copious production of antibodies specific for the invader. Lymphocytes capable of antibody production against the invader multiply to produce progeny cells capable of producing the same antibodies. Some of these progeny cells go immediately into production of antibodies, others become resting cells which serve as the body's "memory" of the invader. If the same (or a very similar) invader makes its appearance again at a later time, these cells are able to respond quickly to its presence.

Vaccination introduces a modified disease agent into the body. Common methods of altering an organism's ability to produce disease are by killing and by "breeding" to an innocuous state. Modified viruses or bacteria are able to induce lymphocytes to produce antibodies capable of protecting the body against disease without actually producing illness. Usually the body produces a higher (usually more protective) level of antibodies and antibodies most specific to a disease agent on the second exposure to a vaccine, but different vaccines vary in their ability to produce a protective antibody level on first exposure. The duration of the body's immunological memory for different viruses and bacteria also varies. These are two reasons why the number of original vaccinations necessary for protection and the frequency of booster vaccinations vary with each disease.

Young Animals Are Special Cases

Additional factors influence the vaccination of a young animal. Dogs and cats receive a small amount of antibody across the *placenta* (organ which communicates between mother and fetus before birth). They receive a much greater amount in the *colostrum* (first milk) and milk when they are nursing. Puppies are capable of absorbing some antibodies through their gut for several days following birth, but the first twenty-four hours are most important. The amount of antibody against each particular disease received is dependent on the level of circulating antibody in the mother. It serves primarily to protect the puppy against disease for the first few weeks of life. Even if the puppy nurses adequately, whether or not it receives a protective level of antibody depends on how recently the mother was exposed to the disease in question or how recently she was vaccinated. The antibody a puppy receives can be a disadvantage as well as being useful since it can interfere with vaccination by tying up the vaccination introduced antigen before it can stimulate the puppy's immune system. The protection puppies receive early in life against canine distemper is an example.

Some puppies lose their protective immunity against distemper acquired in nursing as early as six weeks of age, others as late as four months after birth. Therefore, the ideal vaccination schedule is individualized for each pup. There are tests for determining the level of antibody against distemper in each puppy, but, in general, they are too expensive and time consuming for routine use.

The techniques of vaccination are relatively simple. The knowledge of the proper handling of vaccines and of the physiology of the immune response is what makes it important to have a veterinarian interested in each animal as an individual vaccinate your dog. Vaccination by a good veterinarian also assures that your dog gets a physical examination when they are young, and then later as well to detect important changes that you may have missed. If a veterinarian vaccinates your dog without performing a thorough physical examination something is amiss.

Rabies

The rabies virus can infect any warm-blooded animal, including humans. It causes a disease of the nervous system manifested by changes in behavior preceding paralysis and death. The principal reservoirs of rabies in the United States are skunks, racoons, bats and foxes. Bats and skunks may shed rabies virus without exhibiting behavior which would arouse suspicion of rabies infection. Any wild animal that allows you to get close enough to handle it should certainly be suspected of rabies and be left alone.

Rabies Affects The Nervous System

Rabies is usually spread when a rabid animal bites another, depositing virus from its saliva into the bite wound. However, rabies virus can enter the body through any break in the skin, through the mucous membranes of the mouth, and, probably of the nose and eye as well. After entering the body, rabies virus becomes "fixed" to nervous tissue where it

How Rabies Is Spread

multiplies. Signs of rabies usually begin between about two weeks and two months following infection, but cases have developed after more than one year from contact.

Rabid dogs usually first show changes in their temperament. At this time rabies can be particularly difficult to diagnose because the signs are so variable. A dog may become restless, insecure or apprehensive, overly affectionate or shy. Some dogs snap at imaginary objects. Some dogs have a normal appetite; others have to be coaxed to eat. Some dogs are febrile and have dilated pupils. Following these early signs a dog may become particularly restless, wandering long distances while biting and snapping at any moving object. This is often referred to as the *furious* form of rabies. These animals become insensible to pain and, if confined, may bite or slash at the bars of their cages. Partial paralysis of the vocal cords results in a change in their voice. Convulsions may be seen and may cause death.

The *dumb* form of rabies may follow the furious form or may be seen by itself. It is mainly characterized by paralysis. The dog's mouth often hangs open and saliva drips from it. Since such dogs cannot ingest food or water, they become quite dehydrated. Eventually total paralysis followed by death occurs.

Recovery from rabies is so extremely rare that you might as well not even consider it. Protect your dog from rabies so you will never have to deal with the problem of owning a rabid animal. Dogs should first be vaccinated against rabies when they are three to four months old. There are several types of vaccine available, but the most commonly used type is a modified live virus which is administered by *intramuscular* (in the muscle) injection, usually into one of the hindlegs. Vaccination against rabies is required by state law and state and local laws regulate the frequency of booster vaccination. The current recommendations of the American Veterinary Medical Association for use of modified live rabies vaccines are: a booster shot one year following the original, then booster doses every three years.

If you or your dog are exposed to a rabies suspect, that animal should be confined if possible and turned over to a public health officer for rabies quarantine. All bite wounds should be thoroughly washed with large quantities of soap and water. Whether or not your dog will be quarantined following exposure to a rabies suspect will depend on state and local regulations.

Canine Distemper

Canine distemper is an extremely common and often fatal viral disease occuring in dogs, other canids, and racoons. It is seen most often in young, unvaccinated dogs, but can occur in dogs of *any* age who have not been vaccinated or who have lost their immunity to distemper. The *incubation period* (time from exposure to signs of disease) for distemper is about four to nine days. The first signs are often fever (103 to 105 degrees F), listlessness, lack of appetite and vomiting. These signs may be followed by pneumonia and coughing, sticky yellowish discharges from the nose and eyes, diarrhea, thickening of the skin of the nose and footpads, muscle twitches and convulsions. Any or all of the signs may be present at one time and they may occur in almost any order. If the disease is not fatal, the dog is often left with incurable muscular tremors called *chorea* and discoloration of teeth forming at the time of infection. The distemper virus is shed in various bodily secretions and excretions and is an airborne infection which can be transmitted to a dog without bodily contact with the infected "carrier" dog.

Signs of Distemper

The procedure for initial immunization against distemper varies depending on the immune status of your puppy and on your ability to isolate your dog from exposure to the virus before vaccination is complete. Every effort should be made to keep your puppy away from dogs which might be shedding distemper virus and away from distemper-contaminated environments until vaccination is complete after twelve to sixteen weeks of age. DO NOT allow your dog to play with strange dogs or take them to parks or other areas frequented by large numbers of unsupervised dogs. Keep your puppy in your lap and out of contact with possibly sick dogs while at your veterinarian's office.

Distemper Prevention

Take your puppy to a veterinarian for their first vaccination at eight to nine weeks of age. A good veterinarian will perform a complete physical examination before administering the vaccine. At this time they will also be able to answer any questions you have about the care of your dog.

69

Don't be afraid to ask questions; no question is "dumb" and you may learn something very important by asking. The injection is usually given under the skin *(subcutaneously)* in the back area between the shoulder blades. It is usually pretty painless. If your puppy cries and wiggles when vaccinated, *don't* reward them with hugging and praise which may encourage uncooperative behavior later. If, like most dogs, your dog doesn't whimper, praise them lavishly. Your veterinarian will advise bringing your dog back for a second vaccination in two weeks or more. In the meantime, be sure to keep your puppy well-isolated from exposure to disease. In general, two or three vaccinations are given before immunity is complete. In some cases more vaccinations are necessary. The important thing to remember is that no matter how young when vaccination is begun, a puppy should finish their vaccinations *after* twelve to sixteen weeks of age. If you think the series is finished or have been told the series is finished before your dog is this age, bring them back to the veterinarian's for another shot.

Distemper Treatment   If your dog contracts distemper, a large part of the responsibility for treatment may fall on you since many veterinarians are reluctant to hospitalize dogs with signs of distemper in order to avoid exposure of other dogs. It is important, however, to discuss the problem with a veterinarian and get intensive treatment started early. Treatment consists of appropriate antibiotics, vitamins, and supportive care such as hand feeding, fluids, anti-diarrheal medications and anti-convulsant medication as necessary. Although distemper is often fatal, there is no reason to give up at the first signs of disease. Many dogs have survived severe cases to live out normal lives. Premises contaminated with distemper virus should be thoroughly cleaned; disinfectants containing phenol or alkyl-dimethyl-benzyl-ammonium chloride are effective against distemper virus. Phenol-containing disinfectants are available at drugstores; your veterinarian may have to provide you with others. A susceptible dog may be introduced into a formerly distemper-contaminated environment about one month after cleaning.

Infectious Canine Hepatitis

Infectious hepatitis is a viral disease affecting dogs, other canids and bears. It is not a disease affecting humans. It should not be confused with human hepatitis, although the liver is involved in both diseases. In the early stages of canine hepatitis, the virus is shed in the feces and saliva of infected dogs. Later, virus may be shed in the urine. Urine shedding may continue for several months following recovery. Infection may occur in dogs of any age when they come in contact with virus transmitted by urine, stool or saliva. *How Hepatitis Is Spread*

Canine infectious hepatitis may take several forms. Newborn puppies may die suddenly when infected, without previous signs of disease. Adult dogs with the *fulminating* form first run a high fever (as high as 106 degrees F), then develop bloody diarrhea and may vomit blood as well. These dogs often die within twenty-four to seventy-two hours. Such cases are often confused with cases of poisoning. In somewhat less severe cases there may be no blood in the stool, but signs of abdominal pain, lack of appetite and an abnormal intolerance to light. Dogs with hepatitis usually require intensive veterinary care (hospitalization). Blood transfusions may be necessary if hemorrhage is severe. *Signs Of Hepatitis*

A mild form of hepatitis causing mild depression and fever may be easily overlooked. It may be followed by the development of a "blue eye." The "blue eye" is a corneal opacity (cloudiness) caused by damage to corneal cells responsible for corneal fluid balance. This condition sometimes follows other forms of hepatitis, and, in a very small number of cases, follows vaccination against hepatitis. It usually disappears spontaneously, but may be permanent. Your veterinarian may prescribe antibiotic opthalmic medication for blue eye, but has no control over its occurrence and little over its permanence. *"Blue Eye"*

Vaccination against infectious hepatitis is usually initiated during the series of vaccinations for distemper. The vaccines are often given together as one injection. Yearly booster injections should be given to maintain your dog's immunity. *Hepatitis Prevention*

71

Leptospirosis

Human Health Hazard

Leptospirosis is a disease caused by a particular type of bacterium called a *spirochete*. The organism is spread by contaminated urine which recovered animals may excrete for as long as a year. Rats and cattle, as well as other dogs, may shed species of leptospira which produce disease in dogs. Humans are susceptible to leptospirosis as well. The bacteria enter the body through breaks in the skin or mucous membrane, by ingestion, and occasionally during breeding. Disease occurs about seven to nineteen days after exposure.

Signs of Leptospirosis

Leptospirosis can affect many systems, but the primary signs of disease in dogs are those of kidney failure — loss of appetite, depression, vomiting, diarrhea, increased drinking and urination, dehydration and weight loss. An infected dog may walk in a "hunched up" posture due to muscular or kidney pain. Fever is present early in the disease.

Intensive Care Important

Leptospirosis is a serious disease requiring hospitalization. Refined techniques, such as *peritoneal dialysis,* are sometimes necessary to save a dog with leptospirosis. In addition, the drugs of choice against this disease *(penicillin* and *dihydrostreptomycin)* must be administered by injection twice daily.

Prevent Leptospirosis

Vaccination against leptospirosis is usually done together with distemper and hepatitis vaccination. A series of two doses given two weeks apart is necessary for initial protection. The AVMA currently recommends yearly booster shots. However, the immunity produced by leptospira bacterins seems to be short-lived, and in high risk areas booster doses every six months may be adviseable. Ask your veterinarian whether biannual injections for leptospirosis are necessary where you live.

Internal and External Parasites

Parasites are creatures which are dependent at some point during their life cycle on a host (e.g., your dog). Not all parasites are harmful. In fact, in most well-cared-for small animals, owners overrate them as causes of illness. Certain parasites, under specific circumstances do cause disease; however, don't *assume* that because your dog is sick they have worms or because they're scratching they must have fleas.

If you think your dog has a parasite problem, look for *How to Use This Section* the signs in the Index of Signs (see page 100). (Remember, though, not all animals with parasite infection show signs.) If you find the signs, turn to the appropriate pages and use the information there to help you decide whether or not you need to see a veterinarian. In most cases of internal parasite infection you will need professional help (see page 74). Many times you can correct an external parasite problem yourself.

If you don't think your dog has a parasite problem, it's a good idea to find time to read or skim this section anyway to complete your knowledge of preventive medicine. I've included the information here in the preventive medicine group because the key to a successful fight against parasites is good prevention and control which requires good daily care. If you fail to take into account the life cycle of certain parasites in your general daily care, you may continue to have a problem even though you have administered treatment against the parasite on or inside the dog. Learning about the different parasites discussed here will help you provide a healthy environment preventing serious infection and re-infection of your dog and preventing human infection with certain parasites.

As with the diseases in the Diagnostic Medicine section only the relatively common parasites of dogs are discussed here. They are:

Internal parasites – protozoans (page 74), flukes (page 74), tapeworms (page 74), and the following roundworms: ascarids (page 77), hookworms (page 79), whipworms (page 80), threadworms (page 80), stomach worms (page 81), eyeworms (page 81), heartworms (page 81).

External parasites – fleas (page 83), ticks (page 86), lice (page 87), mites (page 87), flies (page 90).

INTERNAL PARASITES

The *endoparasites* consist of *protozoa, trematodes* (flukes), *cestodes* (tapeworms), and *nematodes* (roundworms). For the most part, the adults of these parasites live in the intestines. *They can be present with or* *A Fecal Sample May Be Important* *without causing illness, and you may or may not see them in your dog's stool.* Only if your dog is infected with one of the larger forms *may* you be able to actually see the parasite. If

73

you think your dog has intestinal parasites but can't be sure because you have not seen them or if you have a new puppy, take a fecal sample to your veterinarian. (A tablespoonful is plenty.) Veterinarians use special procedures to separate the parasites and/or their eggs from the stool and look for evidence of infection microscopically.

Protozoa

There are few intestinal protozoans that cause illness in dogs. Signs of infection, if present, are variable but often include diarrhea not responsive to home treatment. There is no method to diagnose or treat these parasites at home so you as an owner must rely on the help of a veterinarian who can diagnose their presence microscopically and prescribe proper medication.

Flukes (Trematodes)

Trematode parasites are also uncommon causes of disease in dogs. One fluke of importance is *Troglotrema saminocola.* This fluke is host to an organism *(a rickettsia)* which causes a severe disease called salmon poisoning. Signs of this disease, including bloody diarrhea and lymph node *Salmon* enlargement, occur in dogs fed fluke-infected raw salmon and *Poisoning* trout from the Pacific Northwest. Prevent this often fatal disease by not feeding raw fish.

Tapeworms (Cestodes)

Dogs acquire tapeworms by eating any of three types of infected material: 1) prey, offal (discarded animal parts) or uncooked meat, 2) raw, fresh water fish, or 3) infected fleas or biting lice. The common tapeworms *(Taenia* sp., *Dypylidium caninum)* are acquired by ingesting prey or infected fleas and have similar life cycles:

The adult tapeworm consists of a head with hooks and suckers which attaches to the intestinal wall and a body consisting of a series of reproductive segments. It obtains nourishment by absorbing nutrients in the digestive tract directly through the cuticle which covers each body segment. Eggs produced by the adult tapeworm pass out with the dog's feces and are eaten by an intermediate host (such as a rabbit,

74

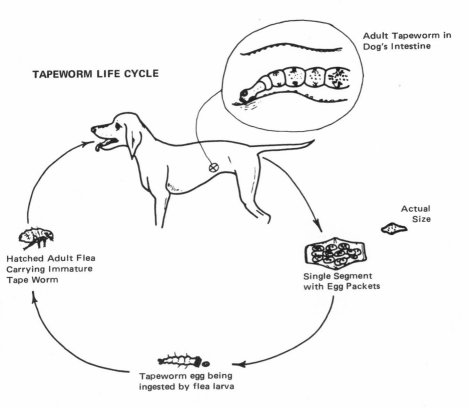

TAPEWORM LIFE CYCLE

Adult Tapeworm in Dog's Intestine

Actual Size

Hatched Adult Flea Carrying Immature Tape Worm

Single Segment with Egg Packets

Tapeworm egg being ingested by flea larva

rodent, or flea) where they grow into an infective stage commonly called a "bladderworm." When the dog eats an intermediate host, this immature form completes the life cycle by becoming an adult tapeworm in the dog. The life cycle of tapeworms acquired from fish is more complex.

Although heavy tapeworm infestations can cause poor growth or weight loss, coat changes, variable appetite or gastrointestinal disturbances, in general you will have no reason to suspect infection until you see tapeworm segments clinging to the hair or skin around the anus or in a fresh bowel movement. Fresh tapeworm segments are opaque white or pinkish white, flat and somewhat rectangularly-shaped. They often move with a stretching out and shrinking back motion. When dry, the segments become yellow or off-white, translucent and shaped somewhat like grains of rice. Tapeworm segments are not always present with tapeworm infection. When absent, diagnosis must be made through microscopic fecal examination.

Diagnosing Tapeworms

In most cases it is easy to rid a dog of tapeworms. If you demonstrate that your dog has tapeworms, most veterinarians will supply you with safe, tapeworm-killing medication which can be administered at home without unpleasant side effects, such as vomiting or diarrhea. Sometimes, however, the deworming must be done in the veterinary hospital. Avoid using anti-tapeworm drugs available in pet stores. Most are ineffective. Effective over-the-counter drugs, containing *arecoline,* cause purgation and can be dangerous. They may cause excessive vomiting, severe diarrhea, and sometimes convulsions. They should never be used in pregnant animals, and if used at all, should always be administered by a veterinarian. After deworming, make an effort to prevent your dog from re-exposure to sources of tapeworm infection. If you don't, deworming may have to be repeated several times a year.

Can people get tapeworms from their dogs? In general, the answer is no, but in certain cases dog tapeworms can pose a health hazard. Small children have sometimes gotten a tapeworm following accidental ingestion of a flea. The second health hazard is the dog tapeworm *Echinococcus granulosus.* Dogs acquire *Echinococcus* infection by eating infected raw sheep, cow, pig, deer, moose or mouse meat so this tapeworm is a problem mainly in rural areas. The tapeworms mature in infected dogs and their eggs are passed out in the dogs' stool where they contaminate the soil and infect intermediate hosts such as sheep or humans. When the "bladderworm" forms in human body tissues, severe disease can occur. If you live in a rural area, try to have your dog's stool examined periodically by a veterinarian and practice good hygiene to prevent infection.

Roundworms (Nematodes)

Roundworms seem to be the internal parasite most dog owners mean when they ask me about worms. Although most people are aware that roundworm infections occur in dogs, most are unaware that, like the other classes of internal parasites, there are several kinds of roundworms. Common ones are covered in the following pages.

Ascarids

Ascarids are the type of roundworms commonly seen in the stool of puppies. They are white, cylindrical and pointed at both ends. They may be relatively small and threadlike in appearance, or as long as four or five inches, somewhat

ASCARID LIFE CYCLE

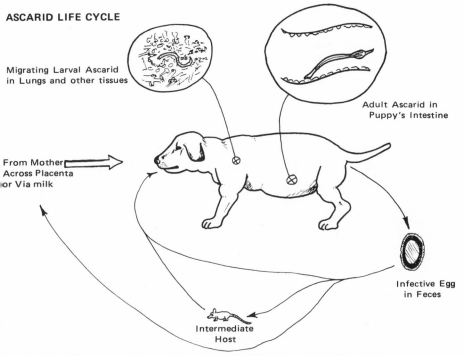

Migrating Larval Ascarid in Lungs and other tissues

Adult Ascarid in Puppy's Intestine

From Mother Across Placenta or Via milk

Infective Egg in Feces

Intermediate Host

resembling white earthworms. Adult ascarids live in the small intestine and get their nourishment by absorbing nutrients in the digestive juices through their cuticle. Mature ascarids produce eggs which pass out in the dog's stool. After about one to four weeks the eggs become infective and contain larval worms. If the infective eggs are ingested by the proper host, they complete their life cycle, eventually becoming adult worms in the intestine. If they are eaten by an abnormal host, such as a rodent, the larval worms encyst in the tissues of this host where they remain unless a dog or other animal eats the abnormal host and releases the larvae.

When dogs over one month of age ingest an infective egg of the common ascarid, *Toxocara canis*, the larvae do not complete their life cycle but become resting stages encysted in body tissues. When a female dog with such encysted stages

Puppies Can Have Ascarids At Birth

becomes pregnant, the larvae are mobilized and penetrate the uterus to infect the unborn puppies. Therefore, it is true that puppies can be born with ascarid infection. Since dogs may have the encysted forms of this roundworm without adult worms in the intestine, and since there are no drugs effective against the larval forms, it is impossible to prevent this prenatal infection by deworming the female before she gives birth. It is probably easiest and best in terms of human health to assume that all puppies have ascarid infections and to deworm them routinely.

Signs of Ascarid Infection
Ascarids do not usually cause apparent disease in adult dogs. Heavy prenatal infection with *Toxocara canis* in puppies can, however, lead to death. This roundworm migrates through the lungs en route to the intestine and can cause a cough or even pneumonia. More commonly, vomiting (of worms, sometimes), diarrhea and progressive weakness are seen. Severely infected puppies may have dull coats and pot-bellies on a thin frame.

Ascarid Treatment
Salts of the drug *piperazine* are used to remove adult ascarids from the intestines. Piperazine is a very safe and effective drug which you can obtain from your veterinarian or a pet shop and which can be administered at home. There is no need to fast your dog before administering piperazine, and it does not usually cause vomiting or diarrhea. Puppies can be dewormed as early as two weeks after birth in order to remove ascarids before they start shedding eggs into the stool resulting in environmental contamination. Deworming should be repeated at *least* once in two to four weeks to remove any adult worms which were immature and not killed at the first dosing. In extremely heavy infections, deworming may be repeated several times before all worms present are killed.

Ascarid eggs are very resistant to environmental stresses. They can remain alive and infective for months once they have contaminated the soil. These factors make it very important to practice good sanitation to prevent reinfection of your own dogs, and infection of other dogs and humans. Stools should be removed at least weekly (preferably daily) and kennels should be built with impervious surfaces (e.g., concrete) which can be easily and thoroughly cleaned. Rodents and cockroaches, which may serve as intermediate hosts for the worms, should be controlled.

Although canine ascarids do not occur in human intestines, their larvae can cause *viseral larval migrans,* a rare condition in which the larvae migrate in the body. *Viseral larval migrans* may cause anything from no signs of illness to severe signs, including blindness. It occurs most often in young children who play in egg-infested soil and put their contaminated hands in their mouths. Although. complete recovery is the rule, the possibility of human infection is a significant reason for good ascarid control and good general hygiene.

Ascarid Human Health Hazard

Hookworms

Hookworms are small internal parasites (about one-fourth to one-half inch long) which attach to the wall of the small intestine and suck blood. Dogs may become infected by ingesting infective larval worms off the ground or by penetration of the skin by infective larvae. Puppies may become infected before birth by larvae migrating in the mother's body tissues and shortly after birth via larvae passed in colostrum.

Migration of hookworm larvae through the skin can cause itching reflected by scratching. Hookworms living in the intestine can cause diarrhea, severe anemia, weakness, and emaciation leading to death. Infection of puppies before birth sometimes causes anemia and death even before hookworm eggs are detectable in the stool.

Possible Signs of Hookworms

Hookworms cannot be diagnosed and treated effectively without the aid of a veterinarian. Hookworms are small enough to be overlooked even when they are passed in the stool. Signs of illness caused by hookworm infection can be caused by other diseases as well. The safest and most effective compounds for treatment are available only through veterinarians. If your dog has to be treated for hookworms, your veterinarian will probably use a drug called *disophenol* and keep your dog in the hospital, or a compound called *dichlorvos* which you may or may not be able to administer at home. Other kinds of safe, effective drugs may soon be available as well.

Diagnosis and Treatment

Hookworms are a problem only in areas which provide an environment suitable for the development of infective larvae. The pre-infective stages require moderate

How to Prevent Hookworm Infection

79

temperatures (between about 73 and 86 degrees F) and moisture for development. If you live in a problem area a prescription drug, *styrlpyridinium chloride,* can be routinely placed in the food to prevent hookworm infection, or your dog can be vaccinated against hookworms (a recent development). Prevent re-infection or spread of hookworms by removing stool in a yard *at least* weekly, keeping lawns clipped short and watering infrequently. (To kill larvae, grass must be kept dry for three weeks.) Paved runs should be hosed down daily and allowed to dry thoroughly. If you keep your dog on gravel, dirt, sand, or bark, sodium chloride or sodium borate must be applied to kill larvae.

Human Health Hazard   Rarely people have acquired intestinal infection with one of the dog hookworms *(Ancyclostoma caninum).* A more common problem in hookworm infested areas is a condition called *cutaneous larval migrans.* It occurs when the skin is penetrated by larval hookworms causing small bumps, red tracks, and itching. The condition is not acquired directly from an infected dog, but from contaminated ground.

Whipworms

Whipworms are intestinal parasites which live in the dog's cecum (part of large intestine) and sometimes cause diarrhea and weight loss. Dogs acquire infection directly by ingesting infective larvae from contaminated soil. Diagnosis must usually be made by a veterinarian since infection is often symptomless. Ask your veterinarian if you live in an area where whipworms are found. If you do, consider having a stool sample examined semi-annually for evidence of infection.

Threadworms

The threadworm, *Strongyloides stercoralis,* is a roundworm parasite of the dog, cat and man. Infection is acquired most commonly when infective larvae penetrate the skin. This can cause red lumps, crusts and scratching. Dogs can also become infected by ingestion of infective larvae. *Strongyloides* are very small worms and will not be seen in the stool. When diagnosis is established by a veterinarian, a drug called *thiabendazole* is often used for treatment. Prevent *Strongyloides* infection by providing your dog with a clean, dry environment.

Stomach Worms

Stomach worms infect both dogs and cats and occur mainly in the southeastern United States. They cause frequent vomiting which cannot be differentiated from other causes of vomiting without examination of a fecal sample and the aid of a veterinarian. You can prevent infection of your dog by preventing the ingestion of cockroaches, crickets, and beetles which serve as intermediate hosts for the development of the worm. Piperazine salts are used for treatment.

Eyeworms

Eyeworms are small roundworms (less than about one-half inch) which live in the conjunctival sac of the infected dog. They cause reddening and irritation of the conjunctiva, discharge from the eye, and, sometimes, damage to the eyeball itself. They occur on the West Coast of the United States and are transmitted through the mouthparts of flies which feed on secretions from the eye. You can treat these worms if you find them by removing them with a pair of fine forceps or tweezers.

Heartworms

Heartworm infection in dogs can be a serious and life threatening problem. Adult heartworms *(Dirofilaria imitis),*

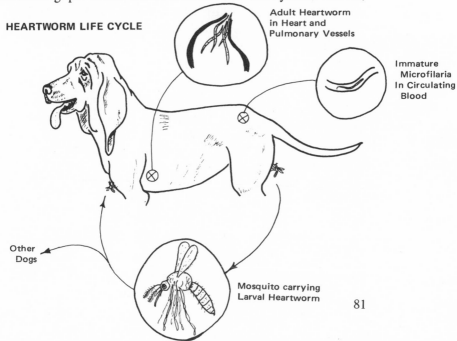

HEARTWORM LIFE CYCLE

Adult Heartworm in Heart and Pulmonary Vessels

Immature Microfilaria In Circulating Blood

Other Dogs

Mosquito carrying Larval Heartworm

81

ranging from about six to twelve inches long, live mainly in the right atrium and ventricle, pulmonary arteries and vena cavae. Mature worms produce *microfilaria* (larvae) which circulate in the blood. Mosquitoes feeding on an infected dog take up microfilaria with the blood meal. After about two weeks in the mosquito the microfilaria become infective larvae which can be passed on when another dog is bitten. There are areas where heartworm infection is likely to occur all over the United States, but infection is particularly common along the Atlantic and Gulf Coasts.

Dogs with heartworm disease may tire easily, cough, have difficulty breathing, and be *unthrifty* (lose weight in spite of good appetite). Signs of liver disease or heart failure may also occur (see page 163). Dogs harboring only a few worms in their hearts, however, may show no signs of disease. Therefore, it is *extremely* important to have your dog checked every six months for heartworm infection if you live in an endemic area. The test consists of having a veterinarian draw a blood sample which can be examined by various techniques for the presence of microfilaria.

If your dog shows evidence of heartworm infection, your veterinarian will want to take a chest x-ray and perform blood tests for kidney and liver function before beginning treatment. Treatment consists of *intravenous* (into a vein) injections of a drug called *thiacetarsamide*. Reactions to the drug may occur so treatment should be performed only by a veterinarian while your dog is hospitalized. Six weeks after elimination of adult heartworms treatment to clear the bloodstream of microfilaria must be given.

Preventing mosquito bites is one way to help prevent heartworms in your dog. Fortunately, a drug called *diethylcarbamazine citrate* is now available as another, easier, means of control. This drug is available from veterinarians as a liquid which can be given in the food as well as in pill form. This drug is only safe for use in dogs free from adult heartworm infection. Be sure your dog is heartworm free *before* using preventive medication.

Pinworms

In answer to a common question: dogs do not get or spread pinworms. The human pinworm, *Enterobius vermicularis,* occurs only in humans and higher primates such as chimpanzees.

EXTERNAL PARASITES

External parasites of dogs are *arthropods* (hard-coated insects and insect-like animals) which live on dog skin feeding off of blood, tissue fluid or skin itself.

Fleas

Fleas are probably the most prevalent external parasite of dogs. They are wingless, dark brown insects capable of jumping great distances relative to their body size. They obtain nourishment by sucking blood. Fleas are not very host specific; therefore, in spite of the fact that there are several

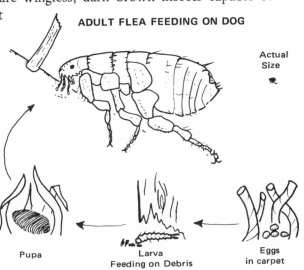

ADULT FLEA FEEDING ON DOG

Actual Size

Pupa   Larva
         Feeding on Debris

Eggs
in carpet

flea species, cat fleas are found on dogs, dog fleas are found on cats, and cat and dog fleas will feed from humans. The important thing is not the kind of flea present, but that a dog should not have fleas. Flea infestation is not a normal and natural condition, and just a few fleas can sometimes be responsible for serious disease. Large numbers of fleas can be responsible for significant loss of blood in puppies, old animals, or any weakened dog. This blood loss *(anemia)* can result in death, particularly in young puppies. Fleas are carriers of disease (e.g., tapeworms, see page 74). Allergic dermatitis is also commonly caused by fleas (see page 104).

Female fleas usually lay their eggs off the host. They may lay them on the host, but because the eggs aren't sticky, they usually drop off. Flea eggs are white and about the size of a small grain of salt. If a dog is heavily infested with fleas, eggs may be found in its coat mixed with flea feces (partially

83

digested blood) which are about the same size but colored black. The eggs hatch into larvae anywhere from about two days to two weeks after laying. Mature flea larvae resemble very small fly maggots. They are about one-fourth inch long and white to creamy yellow. They are usually found in cracks in floors, under carpets, in dog bedding and other similar places. The larvae feed only a little, then spin cocoons in which they develop to adult fleas. Larvae may take from ten days to several months to become adult fleas, depending on environmental conditions. Unfed adult fleas can live for several months.

Since a major part of the flea life cycle is off the dog, flea control on a single host is not sufficient to get rid of fleas completely. Flea control must be practiced on all pets living in a house and fleas must be removed from the premises. Washing or burning infected bedding and thorough vacuuming are often sufficient to get rid of small numbers of fleas. In other cases houses or kennels must be sprayed or fumigated with commercial insecticides or the services of professional exterminators must be obtained.

Home Treat-
ment For Fleas If your dog has fleas, the first thing to do is to give them a good bath. You can use a regular gentle shampoo or a commercial dog shampoo containing insecticide to kill fleas. If you use a regular shampoo, remember that you are removing fleas mechanically only. If you don't rinse your dog's coat well, fleas stunned by the water will wake up as the coat drys and still be around to cause trouble. Once your dog is clean use any of the following things for continued flea control:

Flea Dip 1. Dips are insecticides which are applied to the dog's coat as a liquid and allowed to dry. I think it is easiest to sponge on a dip while the dog is still wet following a bath. Be sure to follow the directions on the package, and be sure the dip you choose is designed for dogs. Sheep dip and other insecticidal dips not designed especially for dogs are often irritating to dog skin and can be toxic.

Flea Spray
and Powder 2. Flea sprays and powders contain a large variety of insecticides. Fleas may become resistant to certain insect-icides so the most effective powder or spray (or dip) may change with time. You may want to ask your veterinarian what they currently recommend. Follow package directions

carefully, and avoid applying powders or sprays to irritated or raw skin to prevent further irritation.

3. The most effective flea collars contain organophosphate insecticides (e.g., *dichlorvos, naled*) incorporated into a plastic base which allows their slow release. Flea tags also contain insecticide enclosed in a plastic cover to prevent its contact with the skin. Organophosphate chemicals act directly on the parasite causing death. Their action in flea collars is *not* due to absorption by the dog and ingestion by the parasite with a blood meal. In the concentrations found in flea collars and tags, dichlorvos has been found to be quite safe, even if your dog were to eat a flea collar. Flea collars can be used safely on *healthy* dogs as young as two months of age, but package directions to the contrary should be heeded. Small dogs and puppies, particularly those with sensitive skin, can wear cat flea collars for an extra margin of safety. Flea collars should be applied loosely (two or three fingers' width between neck and collar) and wetting should be avoided to prevent premature loss of anti-flea effect. Other insecticides should not be applied in the presence of a flea collar or tag unless advised by a veterinarian.

Flea Collar or Tag

A few dogs are sensitive to organophosphates and develop *contact dermatitis* when a flea collar is applied. The dermatitis often first appears as some hair loss and reddening of the neck skin under the flea collar. If the collar is removed at this time, the condition usually clears up with no other treatment. If the collar is not removed, the skin condition can progress to large raw areas, sometimes secondarily infected with bacteria, which can be difficult to clear up and need the attention of a veterinarian. Flea collar dermatitis can sometimes be prevented by airing the collar two or three days before putting it on the dog. Dogs that cannot wear flea collars often can wear flea tags which were developed to prevent contact of the insecticide with the skin.

Flea Collars Can Cause Contact Dermatitis

4. Flea sticks contain a form of insecticide, *methylcarbamate,* in a waxy base which allows it to be applied directly to the skin. As with other products for flea control, follow package directions carefully.

Flea Stick

5. Removal of fleas by hand or with a flea comb are extremely ineffective methods of flea control. Of course, if you see a flea, you can try to remove it, but don't rely on this as a means of routine control if other methods can be used.

Manual Removal

85

6. I have been unable to find substantiation of the effectiveness of home remedies such as wearing eucalyptus buds and feeding brewer's yeast against fleas. If you want to stick to such remedies, examine your dog *thoroughly* for evidence of fleas frequently. And if any are present, re-evaluate your means of flea control.

The sticktight flea, *Echinophaga gallinacea,* is mainly a parasite of poultry, but can attack dogs. You can recognize sticktight fleas easily because the adults stick tight to the dog's skin and don't run off when approached. They are voracious blood suckers and, if found, should be removed by the use of a flea dip.

Ticks

Adult female ticks look different before and after they have taken a blood meal from a dog (males don't swell). Dogs are most likely to pick up ticks in woodsy or rural areas and the worst thing ticks do in most dogs is to cause an area of skin inflammation at the site of attachment. Ticks can, however, cause serious disease — anemia due to blood loss, tick paralysis — and, in some geographical areas), they carry organisms causing disease in dogs *(babesia, rickettsia)* so their presence should never be ignored.

FEMALE TICKS

Actual Size

Empty   Engorged

The average dog usually has so few ticks that the easiest method of removal is by hand. Using your thumb and first finger grasp the tick as close as possible to where its mouthparts insert into the dog's skin. Then exert a firm but gentle, constant pull. (There's no need to twist.) If you've pulled just right and gotten the tick at the optimum time after attachment, the whole tick will detach. If the mouth parts are left embedded, don't worry. The tick never grows back, and only rarely does a tick bite become infected. The site of the tick bite usually becomes red and thickened in reaction to a substance secreted in the tick's saliva, but it usually heals in about two weeks. DO NOT try to burn off ticks with a match or apply kerosene, gasoline, or other similar petroleum products. If you feel you must apply something to the tick, use a small amount of concentrated flea or tick dip, alcohol, ether, or acetone (fingernail polish remover), and apply it only to the tick, not the surrounding skin or hair.

If your dog has gotten a large number of ticks or if you live in a particularly tick-infested area, use a commercial dog dip recommended for ticks and fleas to remove them and act against further infestation. There is no method to prevent ticks from getting on a dog, but an effective dip or spray will kill ticks in four or five days. Flea and tick collars will act slowly on ticks attached in the head and neck area. If you live in a tick area, inspect your dog daily for ticks in order to keep them healthy and comfortable and in order to prevent infestation of the premises with ticks. *Control Ticks With Dips*

To learn about ear ticks see *otitis externa* page 117. *Ear Ticks*

Lice

LOUSE

Actual Size

Lice are much less common than fleas or ticks in well-cared-for dogs. Adult lice are pale-colored and about one-tenth inch or less in length. They spend their entire life on one host, and attach their tiny white eggs to the hair. Some lice require blood or body fluids to live; others eat skin scales. They can cause intense signs of itching and can carry certain tapeworm larvae. Kill lice with a thorough bath followed by a dip effective against ticks and fleas.

Mites (Mange)

Mange is a general term for infestation with mites; it is not any one single disease in itself. The mites discussed here are ear mites, *Demodex* mites, *Sarcoptes* mites and *Cheyletiella* mites.

Ear Mites

Ear mites, *Otodectes cynotis*, live in the ear canal of dogs and cats and feed on skin debris. They cause the

87

formation of large amounts of dark reddish-brown to black wax in the ear, and, usually, vigorous head-shaking and ear-scratching.

How To Diagnose Ear Mites

If you think your dog has ear mites, remove some of the discharge from the ear canal with a cotton swab. You may be able to see the mites by examining the waxy material in a bright light or by putting it on a piece of black paper. (A magnifying glass may help you.) Live ear mites look like moving white specks about the size of the point of a dressmaker's pin.

Treatment of Ear Mites

If you have seen mites and there is not much discharge, you may be able to treat the condition at home. DO NOT attempt home treatment unless you have seen the mites. Other ear problems can cause similar discharges and may be complicated by the use of an ear mite preparation. Treatment consists of cleaning out the ears and instilling insecticidal liquid with an eyedropper or dropper bottle. How often this must be done depends on the product used. Whether or not you will need to see a veterinarian to obtain an effective ear mite preparation depends on the area in which you live. Effective preparations often contain one or more of the following: *rotenone, pyrethrins, piperonyl butoxide, dichlorophene, methoxychlor, lindane.* If your dog's ears are very dirty or very inflamed, it is best to have them thoroughly cleaned by a veterinarian before treatment is begun.

Sarcoptic Mange Mites

Sarcoptes scabei (var. *canis*), is a microscopic mite which infests dogs and which can transiently infest human beings. These mites burrow beneath the horny layers of the skin causing intense signs of itching, followed by hair loss. They seem to prefer the skin of the ears, elbows, legs and face, so early hair loss and crusts are often seen in these areas. Untreated cases can spread until the whole body is involved. *Sarcoptes* infestation *(scabies)* is easily spread from dog to dog.

Signs of Sarcoptic Mange

If your dog scratches intensely and you find small, itchy, red bumps on yourself (particularly on the abdomen), you may suspect the presence of sarcoptic mange. Infection can only be confirmed by

SARCOPTES MITE

88

microscopic examination of a skin scraping and often several scrapings must be taken by a veterinarian before mites are found. It is advisable to have your dog examined by a veterinarian before beginning treatment for sarcoptic mange. Not only can they confirm the presence of mites and give you detailed information on the use of proper insecticide, but a veterinarian can also administer a *corticosteriod* (see page 181) to help relieve the itching until the mites are completely gone and antibiotics in cases of secondary bacterial infection.

If you live in an area where you cannot obtain the *Home* services of a veterinarian and choose to begin treatment *Treatment* yourself, be sure to follow directions on the insecticide *Is Possible* carefully and avoid contact with your own skin. Treatment consists of clipping affected areas on long-haired dogs, bathing, and applying a dip which kills *Sarcoptes* once every two weeks, for a total of three dips. Among the insecticides effective against *Sarcoptes* are *gamma isomer of BHC (lindane), ronnel, malathion,* and *dichlorvos.*

Demodectic Mange

DEMODEX MITE

Demodex canis is a mite that is present in small numbers in the hair follicles of almost all dogs. This mite is often present without causing disease and all the factors involved in the production of skin disease in the presence of this mite have not yet been determined. It has been shown that puppies acquire *Demodex* mites from their mother early in the nursing period, long before signs of infestation may occur. When demodectic mange occurs it may take either of two forms.

The *localized, squamous form* of demodectic mange *Signs of* usually occurs in dogs under one year old. It causes relatively *Two Forms* small (about one inch diameter) patches of hair loss exposing *of Demodex* healthy looking patches of skin which do not seem to itch. These patches often occur on the face or forelegs. This form may also be seen as hair loss around the eyes. Hair loss appears gradually, and after the patches have reached their maximum size, hair usually begins to regrow in about a month. Most cases of localized *Demodex* heal spontaneously. If hair loss isn't progressing, it is usually safe to wait and watch. Be cautious, however; localized *Demodex* and ringworm (see page 106) may be confused, and some cases of local *Demodex* progress to the generalized form.

Generalized cases of demodectic mange may occur in dogs of any age. Hair loss progresses from many small patches to large areas and exposed skin often becomes secondarily infected with bacteria. It is often extremely difficult to treat and can eventually have a fatal course when it does not respond to therapy. Professional veterinary help is needed if you think your dog might have this type of demodectic mange or if the localized form seems to be spreading, since the mites are too small to be seen without a microscope.

Cheyletiella Dermatitis

Cheyletiella yasguri is a large reddish mite which most commonly infests young puppies and may infest kennels. It causes a dandruff-like condition and mild signs of itching. This mite can be seen with the naked eye if an infested dog is examined carefully. Control is easily achieved by cleansing with insecticidal shampoo, or using insecticidal dips, sprays or powders once per week for three applications. Premises should be treated with insecticides such as *chlordane, DDT, ronnel,* or *malathion.* (Avoid *DDT* if possible because it persists for a long time in the environment.)

Trombiculid Mites (Chiggers)

Trombiculid mites (chiggers, harvest mites) are red, orange or yellowish mites which have larvae that are parasitic on dogs and other mammals. (The nymphs and adults feed on plants or invertebrates.) The larvae are often found on the head and neck, particularly in and around the ears, but can infest any part of the body causing scratching which is sometimes very severe. Look for red, orange, or yellowish specks about the size of the point of a dressmaker's pin in affected areas. Use a magnifying glass, if necessary. If you cannot find the mites, diagnosis may have to be made with a skin scraping performed by a veterinarian. Mites found solely in the ear can be eliminated with treatments for ear mites (see page 88). Mites in other areas can be controlled with dips effective against *Sarcoptes.*

90

Flies

Adult flies are not normally parasitic on dogs. Some biting flies cause irritation and scab formation along the ear edges of dogs that spend a lot of time outdoors. This problem seems to be more common in dogs with standing ears, such as German shepherds. If your dog has this problem you can purchase commercial antifly ointments designed for horses' ears.

Some types of adult flies lay their eggs in raw or infected wounds. When the eggs hatch, the maggots feed on the tissue present producing a condition called *myasis*. I've frequently seen maggots in infected ears as well as in neglected skin wounds and under matted hair. To treat myasis, all the maggots must be manually removed, the areas washed with an antibacterial soap (e.g., Phisohex®), and a topical antibiotic cream or ointment applied to treat secondary bacterial infection which may be present. It is extremely important to treat the predisposing condition or myasis is likely to recur.

Myasis (Fly Maggots)

Fly maggots are also often found in dog stool which is not picked up frequently. Be careful not to confuse them with internal parasites.

Value of Preventive Medicine

Begin to practice preventive medicine as soon as you take a new dog into your home. In a short time the way to take care of healthy dogs and how to keep them healthy will become second nature to you. The effects of the lack of preventive medicine early in life can sometimes never be reversed. On the other hand, a dog that is well fed, groomed regularly and kept in a clean and parasite-free environment will have a good start on a long and healthy life. Combine these things with proper training and a yearly visit to a veterinarian for booster shots and examination, and you should find that living with your dog is a simple, enjoyable and rewarding experience.

Parasites Shared By Dogs and Cats

Cat		Dog

External Parasites

Fleas	⟶ ⟵	Fleas
Ear Mites	⟶ ⟵	Ear Mites

Internal Parasites

Protozoa: Coccidia	via environmental contamination with stool	Protozoa: Coccidia
Toxoplasma	via environmental contamination with stool	*Toxoplasma*
Tapeworms *(Dypylidium)*	via ingested fleas	Tapeworms *(Dypylidium)*
Ascarids *(Toxascaris* *leonina* only)	via environmental contamination with stool	Ascarids *(Toxascaris* *leonina* only)
Threadworms	via environmental contamination with stool	Threadworms
Hookworms	via environmental contamination with stool	Hookworms
Stomach Worms	via ingested beetles, etc.	Stomach Worms

Diagnostic Medicine —
What to do When Your Dog is Sick

Times When A Veterinarian's Help Is Needed

Any emergency.

Whenever you fail to diagnose the problem.

Whenever home treatment fails.

For any problem which requires x-ray pictures, laboratory analysis, or anesthesia.

For any problem requiring prescription drugs, including antibiotics.

For yearly physical examination and booster vaccination.

Diagnostic Medicine

General Procedure for Diagnosing Signs

If you have been giving your dog the kind of good care you have learned about in the first part of this book, but illness occurs, you are not necessarily at fault. Even the most well-cared-for dog may become sick or injured. The following pages and the sections on *Emergency Medicine* and *Geriatric Medicine* are here to help you in such situations. The best way to use these three sections, as with the rest of the book, is to read them through completely and become familiar with the contents. In this way, when a problem occurs you will not have to "waste" time in an attempt to digest the new material. You will already know how to deal with the problem, or a quick review will be all that is necessary. Knowing the contents ahead of time will also help you prevent certain problems, for example: *wound infection* page 108 and *poisoning* page 152. Another way (that you will want to use if your dog is already sick) is to start with the index to signs of illness and the general index for the book.

The *Index of Signs* is an alphabetical listing of changes which may occur when your dog is sick. *Symptoms* are subjective indicators of disease. Because your dog cannot describe their feelings in words, they technically have no symptoms, only *signs* which are any objective evidence of disease or injury you can detect. To use the index, first determine what your dog's signs are, for example: you *see* scratching (not itching, your dog *feels* itching) and you *see* red bumps on your dog's skin. Then look up these changes in the Index of Signs and turn to the pages listed to find out about the problem and what to do. If you can't find the signs you see or you can't put the signs into words, look in the *General Index* under the part that is involved, for example: Skin. Use the General Index whenever you want to read about a general subject (e.g., breeding) or a particular disease (e.g., rabies). Some signs are included in the General Index in addition to the Index of Signs. Remember only *common* problems are discussed here in terms of home treatment. If you cannot find what you are looking for in either index, consult a veterinarian. The problem may or may not be serious, but is not one I've considered "run of the mill" for the general dog population.

You should watch carefully for signs of illness. Sometimes a dog is very sick before signs of illness are obvious (even to a practiced eye). Because dogs can't talk, the practice of veterinary medicine is often more difficult than that of human medicine. Since you are closest to your dog, you may be able to notice signs of illness before your veterinarian can find any abnormalities on a simple physical examination. Anything you can tell your veterinarian in the way of signs may be *very* important.

Relatively few signs signal the presence of many diseases. Very different diseases cause the same signs and sometimes can only be differentiated from one another by specialized diagnostic aids, such as x-rays and blood tests. Keep this in mind if you think your dog has all the signs of a particular illness but fails to respond to the suggested treatment. Keep in mind also the value of *intuition* in recognizing that your dog is ill or injured. You are closest to your dog. If "something just doesn't seem right," sit down with your dog, take their temperature (see page 169) and perform a physical examination (see Anatomy page 7). Often you will turn up specific signs which you can read about and deal with at home. If you don't, don't assume that you are wrong and that your dog is O.K. Rely on your intuition and get your dog examined by a veterinarian. They may find something wrong, or can perform specialized tests if necessary.

Three common general signs of illness in dogs are *change in behavior, change in appetite,* and *fever.* Two other general signs you may see are *shivering* and *dehydration.*

Don't take any change of behavior lightly. Although most dogs become less active and more quiet when they are sick or injured (*depression* of activity), any behavioral change can indicate a medical problem. Dogs can have "emotional" problems as well, but you will need to consult other books to deal with such problems at home (see page 39).

Change of Behavior

Dogs may lose their appetites completely when they are sick (*anorexia*). More often, however, you will notice a *change* in appetite. The sick dog may eat more or less. One day's change, though, is not usually important. Watch your dog's food intake carefully. Once a dog is grown, it should be fairly constant from day to day (see page 62). Changes which persist longer than five days with no other signs of illness should be discussed with your veterinarian. Changes accompanied by other signs should not be allowed to continue longer than twenty-four hours before you or your veterinarian investigate the problem.

Change of Appetite

The normal resting dog maintains its rectal temperature within the range of 101.0 to 102.5 degrees F. (For how to take a dog's temperature see page 169). An elevated body temperature (*fever*) usually indicates disease, but keep in mind that factors such as exercise, excitement and high environmental temperature can elevate a dog's temperature as well. Many kinds of bacteria produce toxins which cause the body to release chemical substances called *pyrogens*, that produce fever. The way other agents produce fever is not known, but is probably also related to the body's release of pyrogens.

Fever

It is important to remember that fever is a *sign* of disease, not a disease in itself. Aspirin may be used to lower an extremely high fever (greater than 106 degrees F), but the important thing is to find the cause of the fever and treat it. In fact, there are indications that the presence of fever may even be beneficial in some diseases.

Except in puppies less than four weeks old, lowered body temperature (less than 100 degrees F) is usually indicative of overwhelming disease and the affected animal needs immediate care.

Shivering may or may not be a sign of illness. Many dogs shiver when frightened, excited or emotionally upset. This type of shivering is often seen in the smaller breeds of dogs.

Shivering

97

Dogs also shiver when they are cold. Like people, unless they are accustomed to being outside in cool weather without protection, dogs get cold and shiver in an attempt to increase body heat.

Shivering may also be a sign of pain. It is often seen with the kind of pain that is difficult to localize, such as abdominal or spinal pain. During the early part of a *febrile disease,* (illness with fever) shivering sometimes occurs. The heat it produces contributes to the rising body temperature. If your dog is shivering, try to eliminate emotional causes and take their temperature before concluding that this sign is due to pain.

Dehydration   All body tissues are bathed in tissue fluids consisting primarily of water, ions, proteins and some other chemical substances such as nutrients and waste products. Normal tissue fluids are extremely important in maintaining normal cellular functions. Changes in the body's water composition are always accompanied by changes in other constituents of tissue fluids. Small changes can have important consequences!

The most common tissue fluid alteration seen in sick animals is depletion of body water — *dehydration.* Dehydration occurs whenever the body's output of water exceeds its intake. One common cause of dehydration during illness is the failure of water intake sufficient to meet the body's fixed daily requirements. Water is continually lost in urine, feces, with respiratory gases, and evaporating from some body surfaces (minor in dogs). Dehydration also occurs in conditions which cause excessive water and/or *electrolyte* (ion) loss, such as vomiting and diarrhea. Fever also increases the body's water needs.

Although dehydration begins as soon as water output exceeds intake, the signs of dehydration are ususaly undetectable until a water deficit of about four per cent of total body weight has been incurred. If your dog has visible signs of dehydration, they may have been sick longer than you realize and need professional veterinary care.

Signs of Dehydration (according to increasing severity)   1. *Decreased elasticity of the skin.* The tissues beneath the skin contain a large portion of the total body water. Because this water compartment is one of the least important to the body, it is drawn upon first in a situation of

98

dehydration. To test for dehydration, pick up a fold of skin along the middle of the back and let it drop. In a well-hydrated, normally-fleshed dog the skin springs immediately back into place. In a moderately dehydrated dog the skin moves slowly into place. In severe dehydration the skin may form a tent. (Fat animals tend to have more elastic skin than thin ones.)

2. *Dryness of the mucous membranes of the mouth and eyes.* This may be difficult to evaluate until dehydration becomes severe.

3. *Sunken eyes.* This condition can also be due to severe weight loss, but in any case it's serious.

4. *Circulatory collapse (shock).* See Emergency Medicine page 145.

Mild dehydration and its accompanying ion imbalance can be prevented and/or corrected by administering water and nutrients orally. In more severe dehydration, or with diseases which prevent oral intake, fluids must be administered by other routes. In such cases veterinarians administer fluids *subcutaneously* (under the skin) or *intravenously* (directly into the bloodstream), if necessary. Fluids given via these routes are sterile and of varied composition. The fluid your veterinarian chooses will depend on the route of administration and the cause of dehydration. Good fluid therapy is an important part of the care of almost all animals sick enough to require hospitalization.

When you determine the signs your dog has and have read about their condition, you will need to begin treatment. If you do not already know how to proceed with the treatment involved or need more information on the care of a sick dog, see the section Nursing at Home page 169.

Index of Signs

Pale gums and mucous membranes (anemia) 22, 71, 79, 83, 86, 145

Paralysis 68, 86, 124, 129, 144, 147

Pawing, at ear 87, 116
    at eye 114, 115, 116
    at mouth 118

Pulse, rapid 145
    weak 145

Pupils, constricted (small) 19, 154
    dilated (enlarged) 19, 68, 150, 154
    hazy 161

Pus (see Discharge)

R **Raw areas** on skin 85, 104, 105, 107
    on nose 118

Redness, of conjunctiva (lining of eyes) 81, 104, 114
    of gums 22, 51, 52, 119, 158
    inside ear 116
    inside prepuce 140
    inside vulva 141
    of skin 85, 104, 105, 106, 112

S **Scabs**, on body skin 79, 80, 88, 104, 106, 210
    on ears 91
    on nose 118

Scooting on anus 137

Scratching, at body skin 79, 80, 83, 87, 88, 90, 104, 105, 112
    at ears 87, 112

Sexual attractiveness 140, 188

"Shhh" sound in heart beat 163

Shivering 97

Shock 99, 144, 145

"Skipping" in rear legs 126

Smell, abnormal
    at anus 16, 136
    at vulva, 142, 143
    from ears 112, 116
    from mouth 51, 119
    on body skin 108, 112

Sneezing 104, 121

Squinting 71, 115

Stomach, distended 62, 78
    noisy 131, 133

Stool, eating 136
    dark-colored 27
    light-colored 27, 134
    loose (see Diarrhea)
    loss of control of 129

Skin

In addition to this section, causes of skin disease will be found in the sections on external parasites (see page 83) and nutrition (see page 53).

Allergic Dermatitis

Some dogs, like some people, are born with the predisposition to develop reactions when exposed to certain substances in their environment. Dogs with allergic *(atopic)* dermatitis develop skin disease characterized by signs of itching, such as biting and scratching the skin, when exposed to the material to which they have become allergic. You will see reddening of the skin, small bumps, possibly sticky, oozing areas and scabs, and sometimes dandruff-like scales. The reddened skin may feel abnormally warm to your touch. In neglected cases there is hair loss and a thickening of the skin. If they go untreated long enough, these changes can become permanent. Areas where scratching is severe may become infected. Dogs with allergic dermatitis may lick at their feet and legs excessively. This often causes a permanent reddish-brown stain on the hair. In addition to these skin signs, dogs with allergic dermatitis may have more general signs of allergy such as a watery nasal discharge and sneezing, and excessive tearing and conjunctivitis.

Allergic Dermatitis Has Many Causes

Fleas are probably the most common cause of allergic dermatitis. If you practice good flea control (see page 83), you may be able to prevent the dermatitis from developing or relieve a case which has already developed. Be careful, however, about putting flea sprays or dips on an irritated skin; they sometimes make the irritation worse. If you think you are controlling fleas, but your dog continues to scratch, there can be several possibilities, for example: 1. The bite of a single flea (which you may not see) can cause extreme itching in an allergic animal. 2. Dogs can be allergic to many things other than or in addition to fleas — among them pollens, housedust, molds, trees and wool. 3. The condition may not be allergic dermatitis (for example see page 88).

Bathing Is Part Of Home Treatment

Frequent bathing (about every two weeks) helps control the signs in many dogs and helps prevent secondary bacterial infection. It removes allergens from the coat and seems to relieve some of the skin inflammation associated with allergic dermatitis. Use a gentle shampoo (for example, castile shampoo or baby shampoo, not bar' soap or dishwashing detergent) to avoid additional damage to a sensitive skin. If your dog's skin and hair become too dry with bathing, Alpha-Keri® (one cap per quart water) or some other emollient oil can be used as a final rinse. If you find that bathing makes your dog's signs worse, of course don't continue to use it as treatment.

Often once the itching has begun it continues even if you remove the original cause of the irritation. This may be due to scratching, which releases from the damaged cells substances that cause itching. When this cycle occurs a veterinarian must administer a corticosteroid (see page 181) to control the problem. In many allergic dogs this treatment must be repeated intermittantly.

Skin testing and hyposensitization as used in people with certain allergies has been relatively unsuccessful in dogs with allergic dermatitis. There are veterinarians with a special interest in skin disease, however, who can make an effort to find out what your dog is allergic to in an attempt to relieve the problem. Ask your veterinarian for a referral.

Contact Dermatitis

Contact dermatitis can occur in *any* dog whose skin comes in contact with an irritating substance such as certain soaps, detergents, plants, paints, insect sprays or other chemicals. The reaction looks similar to that described for allergic dermatitis, but tends to be limited to the areas of contact with the substance and is more common in sparsely-haired skin areas. If left untreated, the affected areas often become moist and sticky.

Contact dermatitis is treated much like allergic dermatitis, but long term success is more likely since it is usually easier to find the offending substance and remove it permanently. The first thing to do is to remove the cause. If the contact dermatitis is due to a flea color (see page 85), remove the flea collar. Bathe your dog and rinse the coat thoroughly. Then, if these methods are insufficient to relieve the signs, have a veterinarian examine your dog. Corticosteroids will probably be given and a soothing antibiotic-corticosteroid ointment dispensed, if necessary, for home use.

Pododermatitis

Pododermatitis is an inflammation of the skin of the foot. It is often a sign of a generalized allergic problem, but is also frequently due to local causes (e.g., thorn between the toes.) The web of the foot in affected areas is reddened and usually moist from *exudation* (leakage of fluid from tissue) and licking. It may be swollen. This condition can be painful enough to cause lameness on the affected foot.

Examine the Foot Before Beginning Treatment

Examine the foot carefully in a bright light. Look closely for evidence of foreign bodies. Probe gently for areas of soreness. If you find an invader and can remove it, the pododermatitis may quickly improve. Often the original cause is gone but the problem persists because the dog continues to lick. Washing the foot with a gentle antiseptic soap and soaking it in warm water for fifteen minutes twice a day is often helpful. And try to prevent your dog from licking the affected area. In addition, the application of a soothing antibiotic-antifungal ointment usually helps clear the condition rapidly. (Ask your local pharmacist for the name of a soothing over-the-counter preparation or discuss the problem with your veterinarian to learn which products are available in your area.) If the inflammation and/or soreness persists longer than forty-eight hours without signs of improvement, a veterinarian will have to administer treatment.

Ringworm (Dermatomycosis)

Ringworm is an infection of the skin caused by special types of fungus which may be transmitted to dogs from other animals, people or the soil. Dogs under one year old are more often affected than other animals. The "classic" sign of ringworm is a rapidly growing, circular area of hair loss, but it can appear in other ways — scaly patches, irregular hair loss, crusts and oozing. A ringworm infection can be present with no evidence of skin disease.

Human Health Hazard

Certain kinds of ringworm can be transmitted from dogs to humans. Adult humans are relatively resistant to ring-worm, however, and are unlikely to become infected if

106

normal clean habits are followed. Children should avoid handling animals infected with ringworm because they are more likely to become infected and tend to be less sanitary.

Veterinarians can diagnose certain cases of ringworm with the use of an ultraviolet light alone (a certain type fluoresces green). Microscopic examination of skin scrapings and/or fungal culture is often necessary in other cases. An inexperienced person may confuse ringworm with localized demodectic mange (see page 89) or other skin conditions. If you are in doubt, see your veterinarian.

A cream or drops containing *tolnaftate* (Tinactin®) which is effective against ringworm can be purchased in the drugstore without a prescription. It will clear up a single infected area, but cannot be used to treat multiple spots or very large areas. It is best to combine topical treatment with the administration of *griseofulvin*. This drug is incorporated into new hair to prevent growth of the fungus. Your veterinarian will prescribe this one (or perhaps something better as drugs change) when the diagnosis is made.

If your dog is diagnosed as having ringworm, clean your house thoroughly and wash or discard their bedding. The fungus forms spores (something like bread mold) and thorough cleaning helps remove them to prevent reinfection.

Wound Infection and Abscesses

Whether or not your dog needs to see a veterinarian following a wound depends a lot on what kind of wound it is. Short *lacerations* (cuts) or cuts which do not completely penetrate the skin and most *abrasions* (scrapes) usually need only to be washed with mild soap and rinsed with large volumes of warm, clean water. Larger cuts (about one-half inch or longer) and punctures, particularly those caused by bites, usually need veterinary attention.

Wound healing is essentially the same process whether it occurs by *primary* or *secondary* intention. The wound fills with a clot. The wound edges contract, reducing the wound in size. White blood cells called *macrophages* enter the wound and remove dead tissue and foreign material. Blood vessels and connective tissue cells enter the wound followed by nerve fibers and lymphatic cells. At the same time this is happening, skin cells move in to close the surface defect, and

How Wounds Heal

finally the wound is healed. Wounds which are allowed to heal without *apposing* (bringing together) their edges heal by *secondary intention.* Healing by *primary intention* is more rapid. Your veterinarian tries to achieve primary intention healing by suturing wounds closed. Suturing clean wounds closed also helps prevent them from becoming infected while they are healing. A good example of the advantages of suturing a wound is the cut footpad which dogs often get. A sutured cut pad usually heals in about two weeks in spite of the fact that the dog walks on it. Unsutured footpads often take a month or longer to heal, are sore longer and often bleed. Walking on the unsutured wound causes the edges to pull apart, promotes renewed bleeding and interferes with healing. Unless the foot is bandaged well, dirt and other foreign material are continually ground into the wound, predisposing it to infection and retarding the healing process.

Cut Footpad

Infection interferes with the healing of any wound. Wound infection is caused by bacteria. In most clean wounds the body's defenses (white blood cells and lymph nodes) are able to overcome the bacteria present. In some instances the bacteria get the upper hand. They cause *inflammation* characterized by swelling, redness, warmth and possibly pain, and, if the body is unsuccessful, the death of tissue and pus formation. If resistance is very poor or the bacteria are particularly tough invaders, the infection may reach the bloodstream, causing a *septicemia* (bacterial toxins in the blood) or *bacteremia* (actual bacteria in the blood) and sometimes death. All wounds healed at home should be examined daily for signs of *infection.* Uninfected wounds may show the signs of inflammation, but these signs usually disappear within forty-eight hours. If the swelling, redness, warmth and pain remain or are getting worse or if you see unhealthy looking tissue and/or pus, infection is probably present and you should take your dog to a veterinarian where appropriate *antibiotics* (see page 180) can be administered.

Signs of Wound Infection

Some wounds are particularly prone to infection. Puncture-type bite wounds are among the worst offenders. It is best to leave most puncture-type bite wounds unsutured to allow a site for drainage if infection becomes established. Bite wounds are difficult to wash. Flushing hydrogen peroxide into the wound under pressure (eyedropper, turkey baster,

Bite Wounds Need Extra Care

108

syringe) is one of the best home remedies because its foaming action tends to wash debris out of the wound. If possible, antibiotics should be administered by a veterinarian from the start of treatment (within twenty-four hours of the bite) since bite wounds are so prone to infection. The biting dog (or other animal) should be investigated regarding the status of its rabies immunization.

An *abscess* is a localized collection of pus in a cavity caused by the death and destruction of body tissues. Abscesses are the most common type of infection established fol- lowing improperly treated bite wounds. They usually cause swelling at the wound site. Veterinar-

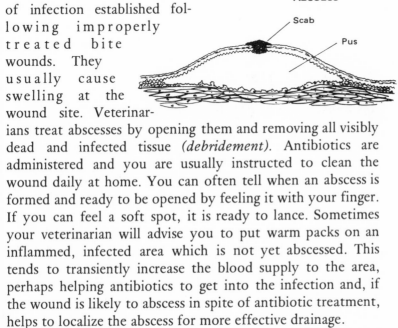

ABSCESS

Scab

Pus

ians treat abscesses by opening them and removing all visibly dead and infected tissue *(debridement)*. Antibiotics are administered and you are usually instructed to clean the wound daily at home. You can often tell when an abscess is formed and ready to be opened by feeling it with your finger. If you can feel a soft spot, it is ready to lance. Sometimes your veterinarian will advise you to put warm packs on an inflamed, infected area which is not yet abscessed. This tends to transiently increase the blood supply to the area, perhaps helping antibiotics to get into the infection and, if the wound is likely to abscess in spite of antibiotic treatment, helps to localize the abscess for more effective drainage.

If your dog has a well-localized abscess which bursts *and* has *no fever* you may be able to get the abscess to heal at home. You must determine how extensive the abscess pocket is; any abscess in which you can't reach to clean the full extent of the pocket probably won't heal but spread or recur and needs a veterinarian's attention. Determine the extent of the pocket by wrapping a finger in a sterile gauze pad and probing the wound *thoroughly*. Be gentle, but be sure to probe to the wound's farthest reaches. A small abscess can be cleaned and probed with a cotton-tipped swab. Clean the abscess thoroughly with hydrogen peroxide once to twice a day (see page 175).

Another common type of abscess in dogs is the *tooth root* abscess caused by an infected tooth usually found in a neglected mouth. This kind of infection may cause swelling on the face; the swelling may come and go. Treatment usually requires that the infected tooth be removed to prevent recurrent abscessation. So see your veterinarian if you suspect this problem. *Foreign bodies* not removed from wounds can also cause a recurring abscess. *Plant awns* (wild barley "foxtails" on the West Coast) often cause this type of abscess between the toes or in the genital area. These abscess must be probed by an expert until the foreign object is found and removed. If you are lucky at home, a foreign body abscess will open and, by *expressing* (squeezing out) the contents, the foreign body will pop out. Infected anal glands frequently abscess (see page 136).

Tetanus is mentioned here with wounds because this disease is usually contracted following a wound which allows the bacteria causing it to enter. Dogs are much more resistant to infection with *Clostridium tetani,* the bacterium which causes tetanus, than humans. For this reason veterinarians don't usually vaccinate dogs against tetanus. Vaccination of dogs that live around livestock might be a good idea because the organism is commonly found in manure and manure-contaminated soil. Discuss this question with your veterinarian. Antitoxin and/or penicillin (which kills the tetanus bacteria) can be given by a veterinarian when a dog gets a manure contaminated wound or acquires a wound in filthy surroundings. Signs of tetanus include progressive stiffness and hyperreactivity, difficulty opening the mouth and swallowing, and rigid extension of all limbs. Dogs with tetanus need a veterinarian's care.

Broken Toenails

Dogs' toenails, particularly those which have been allowed to overgrow, often become broken. Although this injury is relatively minor, it can cause pain sufficient to cause lameness. Whenever your dog becomes lame be sure to examine each toenail including the dewclaw. If you find a broken one, the best course of action usually is to remove it. Calm your dog or have someone else restrain them. Grasp the broken nail with your fingertips (or a pair of tweezers, if necessary) and give a quick, hard jerk. The broken part of the nail usually comes off readily with this motion, and any pain is of very short duration. Bleeding is usually minimal. If bleeding seems excessive, apply a pressure bandage to the foot (see pages 145 and 178) and leave it on for twelve to twenty-four hours. If the claw doesn't come off easily, you will have to leave it until it drops off or have your veterinarian remove it. Broken toenails which are very dirty or expose a lot of raw tissue may become infected. These types of nail injuries should be treated with antibiotics by a veterinarian.

Calluses

Hairless, thickened, wrinkled areas of skin that often look gray are *calluses*. They are found at pressure points where skin closely overlies bone — the elbow, outside surface of the hock, bottom (points of the ischia), occasionally the tail. Calluses occur when a dog lies primarily on hard surfaces. They are usually only cosmetic problems, but they can become infected and then need treatment. You can prevent calluses or help get rid of those already present by providing your dog with a proper sleeping area. Some good bedding materials include foam padding (one inch thick or more), a thick carpet, a thick blanket folded several times.

Puppy Acne and Impetigo

Puppy acne and *impetigo* are bacterial infections of the skin in which you see red bumps and bumps filled with pus. Puppy acne occurs on the chin of young dogs (usually under one year), impetigo on the abdomen. Both infections can usually be controlled by washing affected areas twice daily with Phisohex® (prescription item) or other antibacterial soap or by the application of 70% ispropyl alcohol. Be sure to follow soap washing with a thorough rinsing. Although both infections usually clear up as a dog ages, some cases need veterinary attention and antibiotics. If you can't see improvement within a week of home treatment or if the condition is getting worse in spite of treatment, see your veterinarian.

111

Warts (Canine Oral Papillomatosus)

 Warts on dogs look like warts on people. They are caused by a virus and almost always occur *inside* the mouths of young dogs. They go away without treatment in about two or three months, and should only be removed if they interfere with chewing, swallowing or breathing. Warts are contagious to other dogs so you should probably avoid letting unaffected dogs use the food and water bowls of infected dogs.

Seborrhea

Seborrhea is usually an incurable but manageable skin condition. Cocker and Springer spaniels seem to be affected more often than other breeds. Dogs with seborrhea have scaling skin and abnormal oil secretion. They usually have an unusual somewhat rancid odor which persists in spite of bathing. They often have recurrent ear problems and may have itchy skin. Seborrhea is the dog equivalent of "dandruff" and can be controlled by the use of special shampoos. Some human antidandruff shampoos can be used on dogs (Fosteen®, Sebulex®) for home treatment. I think it is safest to obtain an anti-seborrheic shampoo designed for dogs from your veterinarian (Seleen®, Sebafon®, Pragmatar®, Thiomar®, others). If your dog has a severe scratching problem which is causing hair loss and skin damage be sure to take them to see a veterinarian; corticosteroids may have to be prescribed. Changing the diet seems to have no beneficial effect in cases of true seborrhea.

Hematomas

Hematomas are swellings in the skin caused by the accumulation of blood beneath the skin's surface. They occur most commonly on the ears of lop-eared dogs following vigorous head-shaking and scratching. They also occur on other areas of the body usually following a blow to a skin area which closely overlies bone (e.g., head, side of chest). Dogs with hematomas usually feel and act well (no fever), but you will probably need the aid of a veterinarian for diagnosis and treatment. Hematomas on the head or body are sometimes difficult to distinguish from closed abscesses (see page 108) without removing some of the fluid by needle. And, for a good cosmetic result, hematomas of the ear flap need surgical drainage and suturing.

Mastitis

Mastitis is an inflammation of one or more of the *mammary glands* (breasts). While it may be due to abnormal drainage of milk from the gland, or to trauma, it is usually caused by infection. Affected glands look enlarged, may be discolored red, purplish or blue, and often feel hard and warm. They are often painful, making the female a little reluctant to let her puppies nurse. If you express some milk from the infected gland, it may be blood-streaked, pink, gray or brown. Often, however, the milk does not look unusual to the unaided eye. If left untreated, the gland may abscess or the female may develop more generalized signs of illness.

In order to prevent sick puppies, do not allow them to nurse from infected glands. Placing a piece of adhesive tape over the nipple of the gland will usually effectively prevent nursing. Affected glands should be milked out three to four times a day. Ask your veterinarian to show you how to do this properly. Warm packs applied to the gland seem to relieve discomfort and speed localization of infection. Infected glands must be treated with antibiotics. Your veterinarian will prescribe the appropriate ones.

Pustular Dermatitis

This skin condition which usually affects young puppies is discussed in Breeding and Reproduction, page 210.

Umbilical Hernia

An *umbilical hernia* is a defect involving the body wall which is usually first noticed in young dogs as a lump in the abdominal skin. Its diagnosis and treatment are covered on page 210.

Tumors (Cancer)

Tumors are often noticed as growths on a dog's skin. For more information turn to page 162.

Head

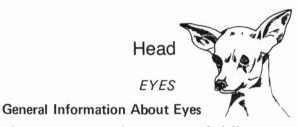

EYES

General Information About Eyes

The eyes are very important and delicate organs. Mild and unobtrusive conditions can become severe rapidly, and many untreated conditions can cause irreversible damage. *Don't ignore even minor evidence of irritation.* Any minor eye problem which doesn't clear rapidly (within twenty-four hours) as well as any obvious change you see in an eye should be brought to the attention of an expert. DO NOT use anything in the eye not specifically labelled for *ophthalmic* use, and do not use a preparation in the eye just because you had it left over from an eye problem you or your dog had in the past. Ophthalmic drugs have very specific uses, and the use of a drug in a condition for which it was not specifically intended can cause serious injury or complication.

Epiphora (Tearing)

Epiphora is the abnormal overflow of tears from the eye. It has *many* causes because tearing is the eye's response to irritation. Among the causes are allergy, *conjunctivitis,* corneal injuries, misplaced eyelashes, and plugged tear ducts. In poodles, in particular, and some other toy breeds, epiphora is mainly a cosmetic problem with no serious underlying physical cause. If you can eliminate other causes of epiphora, staining can be controlled by frequent washing of the affected area and by clipping away stained hair. Surgical removal of the gland of the third eyelid will generally stop or improve the condition in poodles, but it is not necessary for eye health.

Conjunctivitis

Conjunctivitis is an inflammation, sometimes accompanied by infection, of the membrane *(conjunctiva)* which lines the lids and covers part of the eye. It is probably the most common eye problem of dogs because the conjunctiva is exposed to so many irritants. The first sign is often an excessive amount of sticky, yellowish discharge which accumulates at the *medial* corners (see illustration page 19) of the eyes. There are many degrees of inflammation. Very mild cases, with just a slight reddening of the conjunctiva and small amounts of discharge, may clear without drug treatment. Other cases which are persistant, cause inflammation of the lids, and/or extreme discomfort must be treated by a veterinarian to avoid permanent damage to the eye.

In mild cases the first step in treatment at home is to examine the eyes thoroughly to look for the cause and remove it. Dogs that ride with their heads out of the car window or who spend a lot of time outside in wind, dust or pollen, and dogs with lower eyelids that roll out excessively (*ectropion*) frequently suffer from conjunctivitis. Dogs can have allergic irritation of the eyes just as people do. Allergic and mild irritant types of conjunctivitis can often be controlled with over-the-counter eyedrops containing *phenylephrine* and/or *boric acid* used according to directions for humans. Cases with other causes may need to be treated with antibiotics, a decision which should be made by a veterinarian if you cannot get improvement at home.

Foreign Object in The Eye (Eye Injury)

Epiphora and conjunctivitis may be signs of a foreign body in the eye or corneal injury due to trauma. So it's a good idea to examine your dog's eye for foreign objects whenever there are such signs. If epiphora and/or conjunctivitis are *unilateral* (on one side) only, are accompanied by squinting, pawing at the eye or other signs of pain a thorough examination for a foreign body *must* be made.

The first thing to do when looking for a foreign body in your dog's eye is to get in a good light. Slight, but extremely important changes in the eye are easily overlooked in dim light. Place the thumb of one hand just below the edge of the lower lid of the affected eye and the thumb of the opposite hand just above the edge of the upper lid. Then gently pull the lower lid downward and the upper lid upward. This rolls the lids away from the eyeball allowing examination of the conjunctiva and most of the cornea. The surface of the cornea should

EXAMINING THE EYE FOR FOREIGN OBJECT

Foxtail

115

look smooth and completely transparent. If necessary, compare it to the opposite (probably uninjured) eye to be sure the corneal surface is normal. Be sure to look along the edge of the third eyelid to see if there is anything protruding from behind it. It is a good idea to look under the third eyelid, but most dogs with a painful eye will not allow you to lift it without some form of anesthesia. You can, however, moisten a cotton-tipped swab and move it *gently* along the inner surface of the lids and under the third eyelid. Occasionally a foreign body will cling to the swab and be removed, or the swab will sometimes bring a hidden foreign body into view. If you see a large object (e.g., foxtail), you can grasp it with your fingertips or a pair of tweezers and remove it. Small foreign bodies are most easily removed with a moistened cotton swab or a piece of tissue. Any foreign object not easily removed should be entrusted to a veterinarian, and *any* sign of irritation following foreign body removal which persists more than a few hours is reason to have the eye examined by an expert.

I think the majority of foreign bodies are most safely removed by a veterinarian. Since a dog can't tell you when there is eye irritation, it is often easy to overlook small but significant eye damage. Veterinarians use special eye stains to color the surface of the cornea. These stains show the presence of corneal damage not evident to the unassisted eye. Veterinarians also can give local or general anesthetics to relieve pain during examination allowing a more thorough search.

EARS

External Ear Inflammation (Otitis Externa)

Otitis externa is a term used medically to describe an inflammation of the external ear (outside the eardrum). It has many causes, but the signs are usually the same. Head shaking and scratching at the ears are probably the most common signs. In mild cases your dog may like to have their ears rubbed; in other cases touching the ear causes signs of pain. The inside of the pinna is usually abnormally red and there may be swelling. Large amounts of waxy discharge are often present; in severe cases there may be actual pus. (See Anatomy page 20 if you are not familiar with a normal dog

116

ear.) The normal smell of a healthy dog ear becomes fetid as the inflammation gets worse.

All ear inflammations should be treated promptly and vigorously with the aid of a veterinarian if possible. If left neglected, changes occur in the ear which make conditions that could have been easily cured at first difficult or impossible to treat successfully and the infection can progress to include the middle and inner ear. If you are unable to obtain the services of a veterinarian or choose to first attempt treatment at home and don't think a foreign object is in the ear (see below), try using 70% isopropyl alcohol. First, clean out the affected ear thoroughly (see page 174). Then, twice a day, after a more minor cleaning, instill several drops of alcohol into the ear canal and massage the base of the ear to spread the medication all the way down the canal (see page 174). If you see improvement within three or four days, continue the treatment for two weeks. If there is no improvement or if the alcohol seems too irritating to your dog's ear, be sure to seek professional help.

Certain breeds are noted for their predisposition to *otitis externa,* among them are poodles, German shepherds, and spaniels. Dogs with seborrhea (see page 112) often have an accompanying ear condition which can be controlled, but not always cured. Keeping the ears clean on a routine basis is very important in such dogs. Veterinarians prescribe various antifungal, antibiotic, and steroidal medications for use in these dogs as well as for the treatment of acute bacterial or fungal problems. Bacterial or fungal cultures of the ear may be necessary, particularly in recurrent inflammations accompanied by infection. *Otitis* not controlled by other methods must be treated surgically. A *lateral ear resection* (surgery which changes the external ear structure) often cures or improves a condition which hasn't responded to any other treatment.

Foreign Bodies in Ear

Foreign bodies in the ear usually cause a sudden onset of signs of *otitis externa.* The dog will often tilt its head with the affected ear towards the ground as well as scratch or paw at the ear. (Foxtails in the ear are a problem on the West Coast, particularly in long-haired dogs.) If you can see the object at the opening of the ear canal, you can sometimes grasp it with your fingers or tweezers and remove it. When

117

the object has traveled all the way down the ear canal, it should be removed by a veterinarian who can use an otoscope to examine the entire canal and eardrum. If you think your dog has a foreign object in their ear, but can't get get to a veterinarian right away, a few drops of mineral or baby oil placed in the ear and massaged around will often soften the object sufficiently to relieve the signs until it can be removed. Prevent foreign bodies in the ear by checking the hair around the ears each time your dog goes outside, and frequently during hiking. Cotton wads placed firmly in the ears often will help prevent foreign body access to the ear canal if used on hikes in brushy country.

Parasites in the ear can also cause inflammation. Ear ticks *(Otobius megnini)* can cause sudden onset of signs similar to other foreign bodies. Like many foreign objects, they usually must be removed by a veterinarian. Ear mites and trombiculid mites are usually more insidious (see pages 87 and 90).

NOSE

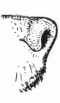

Important conditions involving the outside of dogs' noses are uncommon. Minor skin irritations with signs of raw skin, discharge or scabs are often caused when a dog uses their nose as a tool to dig with or to poke through a fence. You should be able to correct such irritations by observing and modifying your dog's behavior (or the fence). Thickening of the nose skin occurs commonly as dogs age. You cannot prevent this but can help keep the surface soft with petroleum jelly or emollient creams for humans. Any condition of the nose skin (unaccompanied by other signs) which doesn't disappear or improve within two weeks with such simple treatment should be examined by a veterinarian.

Conditions involving the inside of the nose cannot be treated at home. For more information see sneezing page 121, canine distemper page 69, normal appearance of nasal discharge page 30, dry nose page 15.

MOUTH

Foreign Object in Mouth

Dogs that have gotten foreign objects stuck in their mouths usually paw at their mouths and make unusual movements with their lips and tongues. They may make gagging motions and drool, but do not always. Try not to get excited if you think your dog has gotten something stuck in their mouth. Try to reassure and calm your dog, then perform a thorough mouth examination in good light (see page 24). Be sure to examine the areas of the mouth around the molars thoroughly; look under the tongue, at the soft and hard palates and far into the back of the mouth *(pharynx)*. If you see the foreign body, grasp it with your fingertips or tweezers and remove it. If your dog is uncooperative or if you can't find anything, but the signs persist, you will have to have your dog examined by a veterinarian.

Tooth Root Abscess

A tooth root abscess often causes swelling on the face. For more information see page 110.

Dental Tartar

Dental tartar is hard white, yellow or brown material on your dog's teeth. For more information see Anatomy page 23 and Preventive Medicine page 51.

Gingivitis

Red or bleeding gums which may be accompanied by unpleasant mouth odors may be signs of *gingivitis*. See page 22 in Anatomy and page 52 in Preventive Medicine for more information.

Respiratory System

Kennel Cough (Infectious Tracheobronchitis)

Kennel cough is an infectious disease, probably initiated by a virus then complicated by secondary bacterial infection, which occurs most commonly in puppies and young adult dogs. Its common name stems from the fact that dogs often catch this disease when boarded at a kennel, where they are exposed to other dogs carrying the disease or to contaminated premises.

Dogs with kennel cough are usually bright and alert, and are usually eating well. They have a dry hacking cough or bouts of deep, harsh coughing often followed by gagging motions. The gagging sometimes produces foamy mucus. When external pressure is applied to the trachea or larynx coughing is usually easily produced. Most dogs with kennel cough do not have a fever.

The mildest cases of kennel cough may heal without treatment in about two weeks. Most cases benefit by the administration of appropriate antibiotics, which your veterinarian will prescribe to treat secondary infection. Use your judgement on whether or when to go to the veterinarian. Be sure, however, to take your dog's temperature daily if you decide to rely on home treatment. Cough suppressants (children's over-the-counter or prescription preparations) may be administered if the cough is overly frequent and tires your dog. Remember, however, that the cough is a protective reflex designed to clear secretions from the larynx and airways and, therefore, should not be unduly suppressed. Cough suppressants *mask signs,* but do not specifically treat any disease.

To help prevent the development of pneumonia, dogs with kennel cough should be rested and kept in a relatively warm environment. They should be quarantined from other dogs to prevent exposing them to this very contagious disease. Don't assume that any cough is "kennel cough." Use home treatment only if your dog's signs are exactly like those described and there is no fever. If there is fever, your dog is less active than normal, has a decreased appetitite, has discharge from the eyes and/or nose, or has difficult breathing (possible signs of pneumonia), or if your dog is older than three years, a physical examination by a veterinarian is indicated to be sure a more serious problem is not present.

FOXTAIL IN NOSE

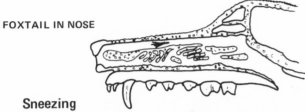

Sneezing

Sneezing is a *sign* rather than any particular disease in itself. Its presence usually indicates a problem in the nasal passages or sinuses. One of the most common causes of sneezing is the presence of a foreign body in the nose. In these cases sneezing is often violent and *paroxsysmal* (recurring in intense bouts). There is often blood-flecked and/or pure blood discharge from the nostril containing the foreign body. A nasal foreign body must almost always be removed by a veterinarian with the dog under anesthesia. (The procedure is not painful, but the "sneeze reflex" usually prevents a good look up an awake dog's nose.) If you can see the object protruding from the nostril, gently try to pull it out. If it resists you, get a veterinarian's help.

Sneezing accompanied by watery, clear nasal discharge from both nostrils in a seemingly healthy dog may be allergic in origin. If sneezing is persistent (lasts longer than three days), the discharge milky, bloody or sticky, and/or your dog is acting ill be sure to have an examination performed by a veterinarian.

Reverse Sneezing

For lack of a better term, this phrase is applied to the paroxsysmal occurence of forced efforts to inhale which produce a loud snorting-type of noise. It is usually pretty frightening the first time you hear it, but most attacks last a few seconds to a minute and cause no permanent damage. The attacks are usually brought on by water drinking, excitement or collar pressure. It is thought that they occur in dogs sensitive to pharyngeal irritation. No treatment is necessary. If the attacks are very frequent and severe, consider discussing the problem with a veterinarian to be sure you have made the correct diagnosis.

121

Musculoskeletal System
(Muscle and Bone)
General Information

Many musculoskeletal diseases can be difficult to diagnose, even by an experienced veterinarian. Proper diagnosis often requires the use of x-rays as well as a thorough physical examination. It may be impossible to distinguish among fractures, dislocations and sprains without the aid of x-rays. In general, however, it should not be too difficult to distinguish the presence of a fracture or dislocation from the presence of a sprain, strain or bruise. Keep in mind that, although musculoskeletal injuries often cause marked signs, they themselves are usually not emergencies (see page 144). Review the musculoskeletal section in Anatomy page 8; read this section thoroughly, and become familiar with your dog's normal stance and gait in order to prepare yourself for an injury to your dog's muscles and/or bones.

When the actual injury occurs, keep calm and proceed with an examination in a thorough and deliberate manner. First try to localize the site of injury. To accomplish this, stand back and look at your dog as a whole. Try to determine the area (or areas) causing the change in posture or gait. If legs are involved, which are they? Which hurt, are distorted or are being protected by the dog. Swelling is often fairly well confined to the injured area, but is sometimes extensive. The posture of the affected leg *may* be fairly normal above, but not below, the affected area. Once you have a general idea of the location of the problem, examine each part of the limb, including each joint, gently and carefully. All legs should be examined thoroughly, but you will probably want to go over the most obviously damaged one first. Review how to perform a leg examination in the anatomy section if you feel unsure, and remember that comparing an injured leg to its (probably) uninjured mate can be very helpful.

Sprains, Strains, Bruises

Sprains, strains and bruises consist of damage to the soft tissues surrounding and supporting the bones usually without loss of weight bearing ability. In these injuries swelling and signs of pain are often quite diffuse. So you may not be able

122

to determine the exact site of injury only the general area involved. If your dog has lameness due to a soft tissue injury, improvement will probably occur rapidly (two to seven days) with rest, and usually no other treatment is necessary. Aspirin (see page 183) can be given to help relieve discomfort.

Fractures

Complete fracture (break) of any of the major limb bones usually results in the *inability to bear weight* on the affected limb, and some *deformity* of the limb is seen. Deformity may consist simply of swelling, or include *angulation* (formation of an abnormal angle) usually at the fracture site, rotation or shortening of the affected limb, or other deviations from the normal position. The sound or feel of bone grating against bone *(crepitus),* if present, is almost always indicative of a fracture. Unless sensory nerves have been damaged or the dog is in deep shock (see page 145), evidence of *pain* can be elicited by manipulating the fracture. Signs of pain, however, are unreliable since it is present in other conditions, since many sensitive dogs overreact to relatively mild pain, and since "stoic" dogs may be less likely to react strongly to painful stimuli.

Fractures are classified as *simple* if there is no communicating wound between the outside of the skin and the broken bone. *Compound* fractures communicate to the outside. If your dog has a compound fracture with bone protruding from a wound, you should have no difficulty diagnosing the condition. Compound fractures easily become infected and should be given immediate attention by a veterinarian, if at all possible.

Compound Fractures Are Emergencies

If your dog is in fairly normal general condition, simple fractures are not necessarily veterinary emergencies. The best thing to do is to localize the fracture site, then call your veterinarian for further advice. Fractures of the foot bones are rarely emergencies and can usually be left unsplinted until x-ray pictures *(radiographs)* can be taken. Whether or not you splint other limb fractures depends on the site of the fracture and the mobility of the bone ends. In many cases, splinting causes more trouble for you and pain for the dog than it's

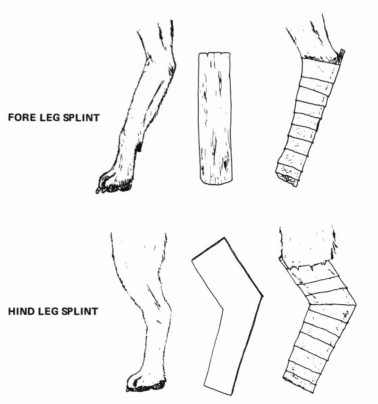

FORE LEG SPLINT

HIND LEG SPLINT

worth. In obviously mobile fractures, where you see the leg
below the break dangling freely and twisting, heavy cardboard cut to the appropriate shape, roll cotton and elastic
bandage can be used to prevent bone movement, inter-.
ruption of blood supply and nerve damage. Compound
fractures should have a clean bandage applied over the exposed bone ends if splinting is unnecessary.

*Spinal
Fractures Are
Emergencies*   A special case of fracture (or dislocation) is fracture of
the spine. This requires professional veterinary care at the
earliest possible time and careful first aid. Spinal fractures
usually result in partial or complete paralysis of the rear legs
and sometimes the front legs as well, often with remarkably
little evidence of pain. If your dog shows such signs following
trauma, immediate and absolute (if possible) restriction of
movement is necessary. If you can get the dog to lie quietly,
transport is best on a stretcher or board. Do not, however,
attempt to tie a frightened and struggling dog to a board —
you may make the damage worse. Small dogs, in particular,

124

can be lifted in your arms if you are careful to prevent back movement. Small and medium-sized dogs can be placed in a box for transportation to a veterinarian. A less satisfactory carrier is a sheet or blanket used as a sling.

The method a veterinarian chooses to repair a fractured bone depends on the type of fracture present, the fracture site, and the age and size of your dog. External devices alone, such as casts and splints, can be used in some cases. In many others surgery to place a metal pin, plate or other internal fixation device into the fractured bone is necessary. A good veterinarian will x-ray the fracture, evaluate all the possibilities for repair, and tell you what they think is necessary to achieve the best healing. If you feel you cannot afford the best repair, they should offer alternative methods which may not be as ideal for healing but more within your means. (Keep in mind that the alternatives may be slower healing or no repair at all.)

Fracture Repair

Dislocations

Dislocations *(luxations)* are seen much less frequently than fractures in most veterinary practices. They occur whenever a bone is displaced from its normal contact with another bone at a joint. *The signs of dislocation are similar to those of fractures, but usually milder.* Dislocations are not emergencies in the sense that they endanger a dog's life or limb. However, they should be examined by a veterinarian within twenty-four hours of occurence because they are most easily corrected without surgery during this period. All suspected dislocations should be x-rayed to determine the true extent of bony damage. General anesthesia is given to relax the muscles and provide relief from pain while the bones are manipulated back into their proper positions. Some dislocations require surgery for permanent correction.

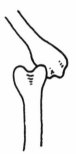

Kneecap Dislocation (Patellar Luxation)

Dislocation of the kneecap is seen most commonly as a recurrent problem in small breeds of dogs such as poodles, Pomeranians, Yorkshire terriers, and Chihuahuas. It results from malformation of the bones forming the knee joint which causes the kneecap to move intermittantly or permanently out of its normal position in the joint. Mild cases cause no apparent lameness or only mild, intermittant lameness, and do not need treatment. Dogs with a mild condition are often described as "skipping" in the rear. More severe cases can cause serious lameness and must be treated surgically. To avoid this problem have puppies of breeds predisposed to patellar dislocation thoroughly examined by a veterinarian before the final purchase agreement is made.

Hip Dysplasia

Hip dysplasia is a deformity of the hip joint in which the joint socket is abnormally shallow and the head of the femur is malformed. It is a complex, genetically influenced

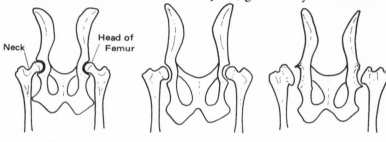

NORMAL HIPS   MODERATE DYSPLASIA   SEVERE DYSPLASIA

disease and some breeds (e.g., Saint Bernards, Newfoundlands, German shepherds) have a notably higher incidence of hip dysplasia than others (Afghan, Greyhound). It is thought that the bony changes of this condition follow developmental changes which produce looseness in the hip joint. Studies have indicated that exercise, vaccines and diet do not change the course of the disease.

Use X-rays To Diagnose Hip Dysplasia

Dogs with hip dysplasia may or may not show signs of disease. Some dogs with hip dysplasia show signs of pain in the hip joint when handled or exercised. Some have an abnormal swaying gait or hop when running. Others have difficulty rising. But the presence or absence of any or all of these signs or other lameness is not sufficient alone to diagnose the condition. The only way to properly diagnose the presence or absence of hip dysplasia is to x-ray the dog's hips.

The average pet with a normal gait doesn't need to be examined for hip dysplasia. However, if your dog is to be used for breeding, an x-ray examination should be performed and the status of the hips determined before any breeding is allowed. The Orthopedic Foundation for Animals (OFA, 817 Virginia Avenue, Columbia, Missouri, 65201) maintains a staff of veterinary radiologists who evaluate x-ray films of dogs' hips for dysplasia and maintains a registry of purebred dogs certified free of hip dysplasia. Registration with this foundation improves the value of a breeding animal. OFA radiologists will evaluate films of dogs one year of age or older, but films taken for OFA certification must be taken after twenty-four months of age because the changes characteristic of hip dysplasia may not yet be present in younger dogs. If your dog's hips are examined at less than one year of age and the signs of hip dysplasia are present, there is no need for x-rays later — hip dysplasia once present does not go away.

Young dogs with hip dysplasia may experience a period of rear limb lameness as they are growing, then be just fine. Other dogs seem to experience discomfort only after strenuous exercise. Most dogs with hip dysplasia develop arthritic changes of the hip joint as they age (so do some dogs with normal looking hips); these changes may or may not cause signs of discomfort and lameness.

Don't believe anyone who says your dog must be "put out of its misery" because of hip dysplasia. Euthanasia should be used only in cases of disability and extreme discomfort which have not responded to other care. If you have a dysplastic dog that shows persistant signs of discomfort there are several things which may provide relief:

Treatment For Hip Dysplasia

1. Provide warm, dry quarters. (Minimizes the effects of osteoarthritis.)

2. Do not allow the dog to become overweight. (Extra weight is just an extra stress on the hips.)

3. Allow the dog to control their exercise. (Don't encourage excessive jumping or forced exercise.)

4. Aspirin can relieve some pain associated with hip dysplasia.

5. Prescription drugs can be used to provide intermittant relief when aspirin is insufficient.

6. Surgery: There are no surgical procedures which can correct hip dysplasia, but there are procedures which can provide relief from pain. The *pectineous myectomy* has been particularly successful in relieving pain associated with hip

dysplasia. This operation consists of the removal of the small pectineous muscle which lies on the inside surface of the upper part of the rear leg. The surgery is a relatively simple procedure. Most dogs I've seen following this surgery are walking much better (often normally) the morning after surgery than the night before it.

The *excision arthroplasty* is a surgical procedure which involves removing the femoral head. It has been successful in providing relief from pain in severe cases of hip dysplasia. It is a major surgical operation and recovery is prolonged (about two months or more) but very helpful when other treatment is unsuccessful.

Intervertebral Disc Disease

The *intervertebral discs* are anatomic structures which normally function to absorb shock and distribute pressure along the spinal column. The intervertebral discs undergo

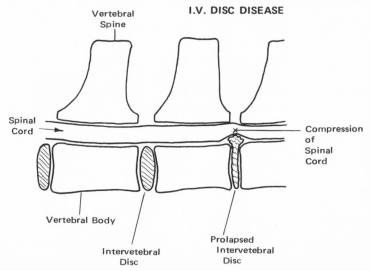

degenerative changes in all dogs as they age and in certain breeds (dachshund, Pekingese, beagle, Cocker, French bull-dog) at a relatively young age. The degenerative changes result in a fibrous disc which has lost its elasticity and often becomes calcified. The outer covering of the disc *(annulus fibrosis)* also undergoes degenerative changes which make it less efficient at keeping the disc material in its normal position. Signs of disease result when the degenerating disc

128

begins to protrude from its intervertebral space, causing pressure on the spinal cord or on the roots of the spinal nerves. What signs appear depend on the area in which the protrusion occurs and the type of protrusion. If you are the owner of a breed predisposed to this problem or if you own an older dog, you should be alert to the possible signs.

Cervical Disc Protrusion (neck region)

Protrusion of a disc in the neck region often causes extreme pain. Your dog may hold its neck rigid with the head in a lower than normal position. Signs of front leg lameness may be present alone (due to effects on front leg nerves which originate in cervical region of spinal cord) or may or may not accompany neck signs.

Thoracolumbar Protrusions (rear leg signs)

If the onset is slow you may see only reluctance to move (e.g., go up and downstairs or jump) or a mild hind leg "lameness." In severe or progressive protrusions complete rear leg paralysis and loss of bladder and fecal control may be seen.

If your dog shows signs of disc protrusion, immediate enforced restriction of exercise is necessary. This will help prevent complete disc protrusion and possible paralysis as a sequel. If the protrusion is minimal and strict inactivity is enforced for several weeks, recovery from a mild episode may occur without a veterinarian's care. Do not be overly concerned with the administration of drugs to relieve pain. Pain relievers often make a dog feel sufficiently comfortable to exercise, causing undue stress on a *herniating* (protruding) disc.

Disc Protrusions Can Be Emergencies

If the signs progress, persist, recur, or the herniation of the disc is sudden and severe, causing signs of leg weakness or paralysis, the help of a veterinarian is important. Cases with rapid progression of signs or paralysis are emergencies. Veterinarians will often confine your dog in the hospital and administer anti-inflammatory and/or pain reliever medications. Medication also may be given to relieve spinal cord swelling which follows its compression. X-rays will be used to determine the site and extent of the problem.

Surgical operations are available for treatment of disc protrusions so severe that medical treatment alone is insufficient. Surgical procedures are also available to help prevent additional protrusions in dogs which have had disc trouble in the past. This type of surgery is called an *intervertebral disc fenestration* and involves removal of the contents of the degenerated discs to prevent their future protrusion.

Physiotherapy is important in the recovery of many dogs with disc disease. Whirlpool baths, swimming, and passive muscle and joint exercise may be given at the veterinary hospital or you may be requested to employ these measures at home. *Paraplegic* (paralyzed in rear legs) dogs can be provided with a cart which supports their rear legs.

Digestive System
(Gastrointestinal Tract)

Vomiting

Vomiting is the forcible expulsion of stomach and/or intestinal contents through the mouth. It is important to try to distinguish between true vomiting and *regurgitation* which is the passive act of return of the contents of the esophagus or pharynx through the mouth. This distinction will help your veterinarian make a diagnosis if home treatment is unsuccessful. Vomiting is a *sign* of various illnesses, not a disease in itself.

Vomiting occurs commonly in dogs. It seems to be caused most often by irritation of the stomach, which veterinarians call *acute* or *simple gastritis.* Gastritis is usually caused by the ingestion of an irritant substance — for example, decomposed food, grass, aluminum foil, paper, or bones. The dog often first vomits food or another irritant material and later vomits frothy clear or yellow fluid. Dogs with gastric irritation may seek grass to eat, but grass eating is often an "enjoyable pastime" for dogs and not a sign of illness. They may or may not be interested in their normal food. If your dog vomits once or twice, has no fever or obvious abdominal pain and is no more than slightly depressed, you can probably treat the vomiting at home.

Home Treatment For Vomiting

Do not feed your dog for the next twelve to twenty-four hours following vomition. At the end of twelve hours (if you can't stand to wait longer), you can offer a very small amount of soft, bland food such as a soft-boiled egg, cooked cereal, baby food or cottage cheese. If your dog keeps this small meal down for about four hours, another small meal can be offered, then another about four hours later. If no further vomiting occurs, the next day's meals can be normal-sized portions of bland food and the following day you can return your dog to a regular diet. Water should be offered only in small amounts at one time. Large amounts of food or water distend the already irritated stomach and usually cause vomiting to recur. An easy way to have water available in small portions is to place ice cubes in the water bowl and allow the dog to drink the liquid that accumulates as the cubes melt.

Antacid liquids (e.g., Maalox®, Mylanta®) or intestinal protectants such as Kaopectate® will help sooth the irritated

131

stomach lining. Maalox® or Mylanta® can be given at a rate of one teaspoonful per twenty pounds body weight every eight hours until the signs have passed. If vomiting is present with diarrhea *(gastroenteritis)*, Kaopectate®-like drugs are best (see page 133). Do not give any preparations containing aspirin.

Times to
Seek
Veterinary
Help for
Vomiting If your dog vomits more than a few times, if the vomitus is ejected extremely forcefully (*projectile* vomiting), if there is blood in the vomitus or obvious abdominal pain, if your dog seems particularly depressed, weak or has a fever, or retches unproductively, DO NOT attempt to treat the condition at home. Even simple gastritis cannot always be treated successfully without the help of a veterinarian, and there are many other serious causes of vomiting, among them foreign bodies, inflammation of the pancreas and kidney failure.

Some dogs, particularly young dogs used to eating several times a day, vomit during the hours preceding their regular meal. The vomitus usually looks like a frothy white or yellow fluid and is usually present in small amounts. This type of vomiting may be due to excess gastric acidity and can be controlled in several ways:

1. Feed two meals a day (morning and evening).

2. Allow free choice feeding.

3. Administer an antacid preceding the time that vomiting usually occurs. This last method is the least desirable since prolonged use may stimulate even greater secretion of gastric secretions.

Another not very serious type of vomiting experienced frequently by young dogs occurs following meals, usually in dogs who gobble their food, overeat and/or exercise excessively immediately following eating. If your dog is an after meal vomiter, you can try the following things:

1. If your dog eats with other animals, feed them alone. Competition encourages food gulping.

2. Feed smaller meals more frequently.

3. Enforce rest after meals.

4. Try a food which has to be chewed before swallowing (e.g., large size kibbles).

Motion Sickness Some dogs apparently become nauseated and vomit when they ride in cars. The first sign of nausea is usually

132

excessive *salivation* (drooling). If the car is stopped and the dog exercised at this point, the signs often subside and the trip can be resumed at least for a short time. Most young dogs with this problem seem to outgrow it, particularly if they are taken for short but frequent automobile rides. If your dog is prone to motion sickness, avoid feeding for eight hours before traveling, stop for frequent exercise and be sure there is adequate ventilation in the vehicle. If these measures aren't sufficient to prevent vomiting, Dramamine® (*dimenhydrinate,* one mg. per pound body weight) given about thirty minutes before car rides will help some dogs. In other cases prescription drugs (certain tranquilizers) which act on the "nausea centers" in the brain must be used to control the problem. Ask your veterinarian about these drugs.

Diarrhea

Diarrhea is the passage of abnormally soft and/or frequent stools. This *sign* is often associated with vomiting, but may be present alone. It has many causes; the most common are dietary. All meat diets or diets containing milk (see page 57) often cause diarrhea. Rich or spicy tablescraps and decomposed food are other common offenders. Intestinal parasites (e.g., worms) may cause diarrhea (see page 73). I see this rarely, however, except in puppies. Diarrhea can be caused by psychological stress such as a trip to the veterinarian's office or new animals in the house, but this type usually subsides quickly and needs no treatment.

Home Treatment For Diarrhea

Home treatment for diarrhea consists of withholding food for twelve to twenty-four hours (so don't be too worried if your dog is not hungry at first), then offering a bland and easily digestible diet, such as cooked lean meat or chicken plus cooked white rice or cooked eggs, for three to five days. (Veterinarians can provide you with special foods for diarrhea.) An intestinal protectant and adsorbent such as Kaopectate® (two teaspoonsful per ten pounds body weight every six hours) should also be given. Look for the cause of the diarrhea and try to eliminate it.

Times to See A Veterinarian for Diarrhea

Diarrhea which persists longer than twenty-four to thirty-six hours without improvement, bloody diarrhea, diarrhea accompanied by persistent vomiting, fever, listlessness or lack of appetite should not be allowed to continue without seeking help from a veterinarian. Not long ago I tried to treat a dog who had been allowed to vomit and have diarrhea for two weeks. Its intestine had been punctured by a bone, and the two week delay, I'm sure, resulted in the dog's death from *peritonitis* (inflammation of the membrane lining the abdomen).

If you decide to take your dog to a veterinarian for treatment of diarrhea, try to bring a stool sample when you go. This can be very helpful in diagnosis and treatment of the problem. The color, composition and consistency of the stool are important, and an examination for parasites may have to be performed.

Constipation

Constipation is the difficult or infrequent passage of feces. This *sign* occurs infrequently in healthy dogs, and, like diarrhea, is most commonly caused by diet. Dogs that do not ingest sufficient bulk or that eat indigestible foreign material such as bones often become constipated. Most normal adult dogs have one or two bowel movements a day, but, since each dog is an individual and diet has a great influence, a routine must be established for each dog. One day without a bowel movement is not a crisis.

If constipation is mild, a change in diet may relieve the problem. Dogs should only be given bones which can be chewed on, not eaten. Constipation due to bone ingestion is *Home Treat-* often associated with crumbly, hard white or light-colored *ment May* stools. Feeding dry dog food will help some dogs who have *Help Mild* trouble with mild constipation since most dry foods have *Constipation* more bulk than canned diets do. Water added to the food may help. Mucilose® and Hydrolose® are commercial preparations you can try; they are designed for humans and are sold in drugstores to add bulk to one's diet. If you find that you must add such preparations to your dog's diet frequently, discuss the problem with a veterinarian.

Mineral oil (one teaspoonful per ten pounds body weight) will sometimes relieve more severe constipation. It works by softening and lubricating the stool. Like all laxatives it should not be used on a continuous or frequently repeated basis. Mineral oil interferes with the absorption of

134

oil-soluble vitamins and prolonged use could cause vitamin deficiency as well as treatment-induced abnormal bowel function. Mineral oil should be administered in food. DO NOT attempt to force it orally; if inhaled, it can cause severe pneumonia.

An enema may be necessary to relieve *impaction* of the colon (hardened stool lodged in colon). This is best performed by a veterinarian, who should give your dog a thorough physical examination before treatment. Fleet® enemas which come in adult and pediatric sizes can be purchased in drugstores, if the services of a veterinarian are unavailable. Insert the lubricated nozzle of the enema into the rectum and administer the Fleet® liquid at a rate of one ounce per ten pounds body weight.

Enemas Are Best Given By Veterinarians

Straining in long-haired dogs is frequently associated with hair matted over the anus, not constipation. The dog sometimes cries continuously or when attempts to defecate are made. If you have a long-haired dog who strains at defecation, be sure to examine their anus before concluding that the problem is internal constipation. Clip away matted hair with scissors or clippers and wash the anus gently. If the anus is very inflammed, a soothing antibiotic-steriod ointment may help relieve discomfort. Prevent recurrent problems by keeping hair around the anus clipped short.

Anal Hair Mats

Straining associated with bladder infection (see page 139), and with severe diarrhea and intestinal inflammation are also commonly confused with constipation. Be sure you know what the problem is before attempting to treat it. (If necessary, insert a gloved and lubricated finger into the rectum to feel the stool.)

Flatulence (Farting)

Having a flatulent dog around is more of an inconvenience than a real medical problem. Excessive gas formation can usually be controlled by changing the diet. Although some veterinarians blame excessive carbohydrate intake, most of the flatulent dogs I see are fed high protein diets (e.g., large quantities of canned meat). You may find that feeding certain types of tablescraps causes the problem. Most dogs which eat dry dog food are not excessively gassy. (Dry cat food may cause a problem because of its high protein

135

content.) Activated charcoal may help minimize flatulence in dogs which diet changes have not helped. Discuss its use with your veterinarian.

Stool Eating (Coprophagy)

Coprophagy is the act of eating stool, either your dog's own stool or another animal's. It is a common problem, particularly in young dogs. Some veterinarians believe that coprophagy of a dog's own stool is due to a lack of certain digestive enzymes and is a method the dog uses to conserve the enzymes in short supply. My experience is that dogs' eat other animals' stool because they seem to taste good. Many dogs eat horse manure and cat feces. The ingestion of cat or dog stool should be prevented not only for aesthetic reasons, but because they can be a source of infection from intestinal parasites.

If you let a young dog know that coprophagy is not acceptable and is disgusting to you, this punishment plus the aging process is often enough to stop the habit. Dietary changes also may help prevent dogs from eating their own stool. Self-feeding instead of scheduled meals helps some dogs. In dogs fed a high carbohydrate diet, try the addition of good quality protein — eggs, cottage cheese, skeletal muscle meat. Diets consisting mainly of canned meat type foods should be changed to include more carbohydrate — the addition of dry kibble is the easiest and most balanced method. Adding the enzyme *papain* to the food will also sometimes prevent coprophagy. This can be done at home by sprinkling Accent® or another meat tenderizer containing *papain* on the food. Veterinarians often supply drugs that make the stool unpleasantly bitter when added to the diet. Ask your veterinarian for one, if other methods fail to stop coprophagy.

Anal Sacculitis

Impaction of the anal sacs, often accompanied by infection, is a frequent problem in dogs. It can occur in any dog, but seems to be most common in smaller breeds, such as the toy and the miniature poodle, Chihuahuas and Cocker spaniels. The function of anal sacs is explained on page 16.

The most common signs of anal sac impaction are scooting along the ground on the anal area and licking excessively at the anus. Scooting is only rarely, in my experience, a sign of "worms." At this stage expressing the contents of the sacs will usually relieve the problem. You can do this yourself. Use one hand to hold up the dog's tail. Hold a disposable cloth or tissue in the other hand. Place your thumb externally over one anal gland and your fingers over the other. Press in and apply firm pressure as you pull your fingers posteriorly over the glands. This causes the contents to be expressed out through the anus into the tissue so they can be discarded. If you cannot empty the sacs this way, empty each sac separately. Place your thumb externally over the sac and your index finger over the same gland inside the rectum then compress the sac between your thumb and finger.

If impacted anal sacs are not emptied, one or both may *Anal Sac* become infected. Infected sacs are usually painful, and you *Abscesses* may be able to express blood-tinged material or pus from the sac. If you don't notice the infection at this stage, you may later see an abscess or swelling externally at one side or the other of the anus. The abscess may open and drain to the outside. Infected anal sacs are best treated by a veterinarian. If they have not yet abscessed, it may be possible to treat them with antibiotics alone. If they are abscessed surgical drainage is usually necessary. Chronically inflamed and/or infected anal sacs may have to be removed.

Hiccups

Hiccups which occur in dogs are the same as those people have. They are caused by a sporadic contraction of the diaphragm. Hiccups are seen most often in puppies and usually stop spontaneously without treatment. A dog with continuous hiccups which don't stop spontaneously within twenty-four hours needs to be examined by a veterinarian.

Obesity

Obesity (fatness) is almost always an owner-induced disease in dogs caused by overfeeding. Excessive fat puts excessive stresses on your dog's joints, heart and lungs and often results in an inactive dog that is a poor companion. An obese dog, as you may have discovered, is more difficult to examine thoroughly than a normally-fleshed one, since excess fat interferes with listening to or feeling the heart beat and with feeling the pulse and abdominal organs. An obese dog is a poorer surgical risk. If your dog is overweight, have them examined by a veterinarian if you want to be sure that their general health is good and that their condition is not caused by an hormonal imbalance (this requires blood tests), then put them on a diet.

Desired Weight	Daily Maintenance Calorie Requirement
5 lbs	250
10 lbs	420
15 lbs	525
20 lbs	700
30 lbs	960
40 lbs	1280
50 lbs	1550
60 lbs	1800
70 lbs	2100
80 lbs	2400
90 lbs	2700
100 lbs	3000

Choose the weight you want your dog to reduce to. Then feed fifty to sixty percent of the daily Calorie requirement to maintain that weight until the desired weight is reached. This could take several months. You can use the following as a guide to how much commercial food will provide the proper amount of Calories:

Type of Food	Calories Per Pound Food
Dry food	1500
Semi-moist	1350
Canned *complete* diet	500

If you make your dog's food, you will have to determine the Calorie content yourself. You can feed the calculated amount of food in as many meals as you desire each day, but, remember, *more food is not allowed.* If your dog is accustomed to begging and you can't resist, offer small pieces of raw vegetable such as carrots or a clean bone to chew on.

Weigh your dog weekly. If you are following the rules set out above and your dog is not losing weight, consult your veterinarian for further help. Once your dog has reached the desired weight, you can relax the rules a little to increase your dog's Calorie intake to the maintenance level for that weight. Weigh your dog once a month thereafter and make small adjustments in the diet whenever your dog starts to gain weight.

An example: Your dog weighs thirty pounds, but should weigh twenty. The daily maintenance Calorie requirement for a twenty pound dog is about 700 Calories x 60% = 420 Calories to be fed while reducing. This is about thirteen ounces of canned complete diet, four and one-half ounces of dry food, or five ounces of semi-moist food to be fed until the desired weight is reached. When the desired weight of twenty pounds is reached the food intake could be raised to about twenty ounces of canned complete diet, seven and one-half ounces dry food or eight and four-tenths ounces semi-moist food.

Genitourinary System

General Information

If your dog has any of the following signs, *genitourinary* (reproductive or urinary) system disease may be present and immediate, thorough examination by a veterinarian is indicated:

Drinking increased amounts of water
Urinating very frequently
Urinating abnormally large or small amounts
Difficulty or inability to urinate
Bloody urine
Blood and or pus-like material dripping in quantity from penis or vulva
Abdominal pain or walking with an arched back

Balanoposthitis (Inflammation of Penis)

A small amount of opaque white or yellowish discharge from the *prepuce* (skin covering penis) is present in almost all mature male dogs, and is generally considered normal. When this discharge is excessive, perhaps greenish or odorous, and the dogs licks at his prepuce excessively, these are signs of an inflammation of the lining of the prepuce and the surface of the penis veterinarians call *balanoposthitis.* If you protrude the penis (see page 28) and examine its surface and the lining of the sheath, you may see small, smooth lumps which are enlarged *lymphoid follicles* and the surface of the penis may look abnormally red. You should look for foreign material, such as foxtails, inside the prepuce as well. If you see one and remove it, your dog's problem may be solved without the aid of a veterinarian. Simple balanoposthistis without the presence of a foreign body is treated by flushing the prepuce with antibiotic solutions or ointments which your veterinarian can prescribe if you cannot find an obvious cause and get rid of it.

Vaginitis

Vaginitis is an inflammation, often with accompanying infection, of the vagina similar to the vaginal inflammation common in humans. Females with vaginitis have a sticky, yellowish, greenish or grey discharge often seen on the hairs at the vulva. They may lick excessively at their vulva and may be unusually sexually attractive to male dogs. If you examine the mucous membrane (skin) inside the lips of the vulva, you may find it abnormally red or bumpy.

Vaginitis in females who have not yet reached puberty may be characterized by a small amount of discharge only, and often does not need treatment. It usually disappears at the time of first heat. If your young female has only mild signs at the vulva and seems generally healthy you may choose to wait on treatment.

Vaginitis in older females should always be examined by a veterinarian because more serious diseases, such as *pyometra* (see page 143), can be confused with it. It is treated by the use of antibiotics, sometimes douching, suppositories, and estrogen hormones. Vaginitis in both puppies and adult females may be accompanied by a bladder infection *(cystitis)*.

Cystitis (Bladder Infection)

Cystitis is an inflammation of the bladder most often caused by bacterial infection. It can occur in both male and female dogs, but is more common in females. Dogs with cystitis often urinate very frequently or strain to urinate frequently without passing much urine. (This sometimes causes cystitis to be confused with constipation.) The urine may look normal to you or it can appear cloudy or bloody. Females with cystitis may lick at their vulvas excessively and may have a vaginal discharge. Cystitis may also be due to causes other than bacterial infection, such as bladder tumors or stones.

If you think your dog may have cystitis, immediate examination by a veterinarian is indicated. They will want to perform a urinalysis, so you can help by bringing a clean, recently caught urine sample with you. To obtain a clean urine sample, begin with a clean, dry jar, pan or pie tin. Wash your dog's genital area with mild soap and rinse with lots of clear water, then dry. Take your dog outdoors on a leash and, when the dog squats or lifts its leg to urinate, slip the pan quickly into the stream to catch the urine. You only need to catch about one-fourth cup of urine for a complete urinalysis. Transfer the urine to a clean container and take it in for analysis within the hour. If you will have to wait longer

How to Obtain A Urine Sample

141

than an hour, refrigerate the urine. If you can plan ahead, ask your veterinarian to provide you with a urine container and preservative if necessary. Try not to contaminate the urine with hair, dirt, grass or other foreign materials.

If your veterinarian finds evidence of bladder infection in the clean sample, they will probably want to take a sterile sample for bacterial culture. This helps determine the preferred drugs for treatment. After your dog is treated, you will want your veterinarian to examine another urine sample — sometimes signs of cystitis disappear after treatment even though the infection is still present. Abdominal x-rays may be necessary, particularly if your veterinarian suspects more than a simple bacterial infection. It is extremely important that cystitis be treated promptly and properly to prevent retrograde infection of the kidneys and other possible permanent damage to the urinary system. (For more information on urinary tract disease see page 160).

Swelling of Vulva

Normal swelling of the vulva precedes the onset of heat often by as much as a month and occasionally more. This change in the vulva can be recognized only if you become familiar with the appearance of your dog's vulva while she is in the *anestrous* state (see page 188). Other swelling in the genital area is uncommon. Foreign body abscesses sometimes occur in this region, however (see page 110). If you cannot find an obvious cause of swelling and don't think the time of your female's heat is near, be sure to have her examined by a veterinarian.

Bleeding at Vulva (Proestrus)

Proestrus is the time during which a bloody discharge first appears at the vulva of the sexually mature female. For more information see page 188. If your female dog is not "in heat," any bloody vulvar discharge should be cause for examination by a veterinarian.

Estrus (Mating Readiness)

For signs of mating readiness see page 196.

False Pregnancy

For signs of false pregnancy see page 197.

Uterine Infection

Pyometra is a type of uterine infection which occurs *Pyometra* most commonly in older unspayed (or partially spayed, see page 192) females. It usually occurs following estrus and is probably due to a hormonal imbalance. In cases of pyometra where the cervix is open there is usually a sticky reddish to yellow, abnormal smelling discharge from the vulva. *Other cases have no discharge.* A female with pyometra is often listless, lacks appetite and shows increased water intake and increased urination. She may vomit and *sometimes* has fever. If not treated, this condition can cause death. Ovario-hysterectomy is the treatment of choice for pyometra. In rare instances of pyometra in valuable breeding animals methods other than spaying have been used. Females with pyometra are much poorer surgical risks than healthy young dogs so consider having an ovariohysterectomy (see page 189) performed when your dog is young, and rush your dog to a veterinarian if your think pyometra may be present.

A retained placenta or fetus, or a lack of cleanliness *Acute* during delivery can result in an infection of the uterus later, *Metritis* *acute metritis.* A female with acute metritis is usually depressed, febrile, lacks appetite and may seem uninterested in her puppies. She may seem excessively thirsty, vomit and/or have diarrhea. The discharge from the vulva is often odorous, reddish and watery, or later dark brown and pus-like. This condition calls for immediate treatment by a veterinarian. Puppies may have to be raised by hand (see page 205) since females with acute metritis often do not have enough milk, or the milk produced may be toxic.

143

Emergency Medicine

General Information

An *emergency* is any situation which requires immediate action in order to prevent irreversible damage to or death of your dog. Each of the following signs indicates an emergency situation:

Uncontrollable bleeding

Extreme difficulty breathing

Continuous or recurrent convulsions

Unconsciousness

Shock

Sudden paralysis

Repeated or continuous vomiting and/or diarrhea

Conditions such as injury to the eyeball or snakebite are usually emergencies; others, such as possible leg injuries, are not so clear cut. Therefore, in many cases you will have to use your intuition to make a good judgement about the best action to take.

It is to both you and your veterinarian's benefit that you can accurately recognize an emergency. No veterinarian I know enjoys being taken away from dinner, pulled from the bathtub or awakened in the middle of the night by an hysterical pet owner who obviously does not have an emergency. Most veterinarians value their leisure time more than any emergency fee they may collect. Rational pet owners are often unhappy to find out upon reaching the veterinary hospital that the "emergency" could have safely waited until morning and that the emergency fee could have been saved. Usually getting emotionally upset leads to restricted judgement. Try to remain calm and use this section as a reference.

Most emergencies I see are the result of trauma (hit by a car, dog fights) or poisoning. Most could have easily been prevented if the owner had confined their dog to a yard or run when unable to supervise them. Medical emergencies due to failure of a vital organ could often have been prevented by consulting a veterinarian soon after the earlier signs appeared. Look ahead. If a weekend or holiday is coming up, it may be a good idea to take your dog in for an examination even if the signs seem minor.

Shock

The term *shock* is one I hear frequently abused. It is extremely important to know whether or not shock is truly present, because its presence or absence often determines whether or not a condition is an emergency. Shock can be simply defined as *the failure of the cardiovascular system to provide the body tissues with oxygen.* There are several causes of shock; the most common in veterinary medicine is blood loss. The following are signs which may indicate the presence of shock:

1. Depression (quietness and inactivity) and lack of normal response to external environmental stimuli.

2. Rapid heart and respiratory rate.

3. Poor capillary refilling time. To test for capillary refilling time, press firmly against the gums, causing them to blanch (whiten) beneath your finger. Lift your finger away and see how long it takes for the color to return to the blanched area. The normal refilling time is no more than one or two seconds. Poor capillary filling is an early and constant sign in shock. It precedes the pale, cool mucous membranes present in advanced shock.

4. Rapid pulse which becomes weak and may become absent as shock progresses.

5. Lowered body temperature. The extremities (legs and paws) and skin become cool to the touch, and rectal temperature often drops below 100 degrees F.

If your dog shows signs of shock following injury or prolonged illness, contact a veterinarian immediately. But first wrap your dog in a towel or blanket (if available) to preserve body heat.

Signs of Shock, Progressively Serious

External Bleeding and How to Stop It (Hemostasis)

Most cuts through the skin will stop bleeding within five or six minutes of their occurence. Those which do not or which are bleeding profusely need some kind of immediate care, especially if it's going to be a while before you can enlist professional veterinary aid.

A *pressure bandage* is the best way to stop bleeding. If a gauze pad is available, place this directly over the wound; then apply the bandage over it. Any clean strip of material can be used for a bandage. Gauze roller bandage, a strip of

Pressure Bandage

145

APPLYING A PRESSURE BANDAGE TO THE TAIL

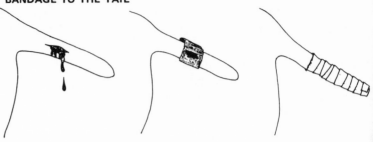

sheet or an elastic bandage are best since persistent bleeding causes seepage which you can see through such bandages. If the wound is on the trunk or you only plan to bandage a limb temporarily, apply several wraps of bandage *firmly* directly over the wound. If the bandage is to be left on a limb for several hours or more, it should be applied over the wound and down the leg to cover the foot as well. This will prevent swelling and *ischemia* (lack of blood) of the part of the limb below the bandage. This rule applies to bandaging the tail as well. If you cannot apply a pressure bandage, firm, *direct pressure* (with your bare hand, if necessary) over the wound for several minutes will often stop bleeding.

If a pressure bandage will successfully stop the bleeding and no other problems are apparent, you can usually wait until the next day to have the wound examined and treated by a veterinarian. Most wounds severe enough to require a pressure bandage will need *suturing* (sewing closed) for proper and most rapid healing. (Any wound which gapes open is likely to benefit from suturing.)

A *tourniquet* is a second and *much less desirable* method of *hemostasis.* Tourniquets are useful only for bleeding involving a limb or the tail, and should be loosened *at least* every fifteen minutes to allow reoxygenation of tissues. Use any strong cord, rope or bandage strip to form a tourniquet. Form a loop and apply it on the extremity between the body and the wound. (It is easiest to apply it at a joint to prevent slippage.) Watch the change in blood flow to

TOURNIQUET

146

determine how tightly to tie the tourniquet. Proper application will usually cause an immediate and definite slowing of blood seepage. When you achieve sufficient slowing, stop tightening the tourniquet. Then consider replacing the tourniquet with a pressure bandage if at all possible.

Hit By Car

The first thing to do if you find your dog hit by a car is to try to remain calm. This isn't easy since your animal is so important to you, but hysterics will not help you or your *Remain Calm* dog. Try to assess the damage that has been done. You must gather information to help your veterinarian decide the seriousness of the injuries before you get to the hospital. So concentrate your attention on this plan of action while administering first aid.

Many seriously injured animals try to run from the scene of their accident in fright, thereby increasing the injuries or becoming lost and unavailable for veterinary care. DO NOT leave your dog unattended for one second. If necessary ask a bystander to telephone your veterinarian, or carry your animal with you to the telephone. (Before moving check for possible fractures or spinal cord damage. See below.)

First, evaluate your dog for signs of shock. A fracture or *Look For Signs* large cut can be spectacular and frightening, but this matter *of Shock* takes secondary consideration. If signs of shock are present, be sure your dog gets professional veterinary care at once.

A small amount of blood can appear to be more than it *External and* is. Try to determine the source of the blood loss. When you *Internal Bleeding* find the site, you often find that the original bleeding has stopped. If there is a great deal of bleeding from the wound, apply a makeshift pressure bandage or direct pressure to it (see page 145). Persistant bleeding from the nose and/or mouth requires immediate veterinary care as does blood in the urine or signs that indicate internal bleeding and/or injury (shock, abdominal pain, difficult breathing).

A veterinarian should be consulted if you think your *Fractures* dog has a fractured limb, but the fracture itself may not be an emergency if the dog is doing well otherwise (see page 123). *Paralysis or partial paralysis may indicate spinal cord damage* and requires that you keep the vertebral column as immobile as possible from the time of the accident until you arrive at the veterinary hospital (see page 124). A nose muzzle (see page 178) is important to protect yourself if the animal is frightened and uncooperative. A stretcher or board is the best means to carry a severely injured dog. If you can't determine the extent of injury or do not have a makeshift stretcher available, carry the dog in one of the following ways:

CARRYING THE DOG

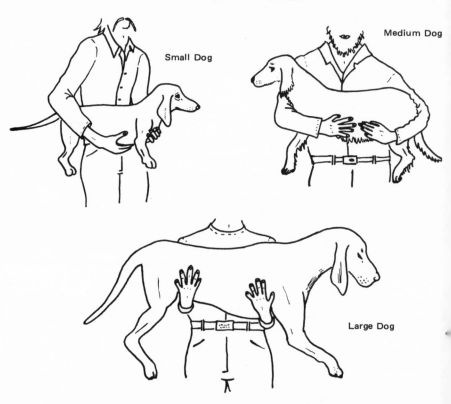

Small Dog

Medium Dog

Large Dog

Internal Injuries   If you find that your dog seems essentially normal following the accident, you may not need to see a veterinarian. You should be aware, however, that certain major internal injuries may not be apparent for several hours (sometimes days) following such trauma:

148

A *diaphragmatic hernia* results when a tear in the *Diaphragmatic Hernia* diaphragm allows abdominal organs to move through it into the chest. If the tear occurs at the time of an accident, but the actual hernia does not (or is mild) you may not see any signs. When the abdominal organs herniate (or a small hernia gets worse) strained respiration ensues. Lack of appetite, difficulty swallowing or vomiting may be seen. If you try to hear the heart sounds, they may be absent or muffled. If a large portion of the abdominal organs have moved into the chest, you may notice a "tucked up" abdomen. Watch for signs indicating possible diaphragmatic hernia for several weeks following any severe accident.

Be sure to watch for signs of normal urination following *Ruptured Bladder* incidents involving abdominal trauma, such as that suffered when a dog is hit by a car. Dogs with ruptured bladders may act normally at first then later develop abdominal pain. Their abdomens may be very tender when examined. If urination is completely absent or blood-stained or if normal looking urine is passed with some difficulty, suspect a ruptured bladder which is a surgical emergency.

If your dog is not examined by a veterinarian following an accident be sure to give them a thorough physical examination yourself, and watch them closely for signs of shock for twenty-four hours. Don't forget to examine the abdomen thoroughly by palpation. If your dog shows signs of pain such as *tensing* (contracting) the abdominal muscles more than usual or crying out, or if the abdomen feels unusual to you (too few, too many, or unusually shaped masses present), be sure to arrange for an examination by a veterinarian.

Artificial Respiration

Any occasion in which you have to resort to artificial respiration is an emergency (except perhaps in a newborn puppy that is slow to start breathing). Don't spend all your time trying to revive the dog on the spot. As soon as your veterinarian is contacted, head for the clinic while continuing attempts at resuscitation. Artificial respiration serves no purpose in an already dead animal. Place your ear on the *Signs of Death* unconscious dog's chest and listen for a heart beat; feel for a pulse (see page 32). If no pulse of heart beat are detectable

149

and the pupils are dilated and nonresponsive to light, it is probable that death has already occurred and that your first aid will be useless.

To administer artificial respiration, open the mouth, pull out the tongue and look as far back into the pharynx as possible to visualize any obstructions that may be present. If you can't see anything, it is a good idea to feel for obstructions with your fingers. Wipe away excessive mucous or blood in the pharynx that might interfere with air flow. Then close the dog's mouth. Inhale. Holding the dog's mouth closed, place your mouth over their nose (cover it completely) and exhale in an attempt to force the exhaled air through the dog's nose into the chest. In small dogs your mouth may cover the whole *anterior*

ARTIFICIAL RESPIRATION

(front) part of the muzzle. Then watch for the chest to expand as you blow. After inflating the lungs in this manner, remove your mouth to allow the chest to return to its original (deflated) position. Repeat the inflation-deflation cycle about six times per minute as long as necessary.

External Heart Massage

External heart massage is used in an attempt to maintain circulation when cardiac arrest has occurred. If you cannot feel a pulse or heart beat in an unconscious and

EXTERNAL HEART MASSAGE

non-breathing dog, you may try external cardiac massage. Heart arrest automatically follows respiratory arrest, or when heart arrest occurs first, breathing soon stops. Therefore, *cardiac massage must be combined with artificial respiration if any benefit is to be gained.* Irreversible damage to the brain

150

is said to occur after three minutes without oxygen. This implys that heart massage must be started within three to five minutes following cardiac arrest to be of benefit.

Place the dog on its right side on a firm surface. Place the hands over the heart on the left side of the chest and compress it firmly. (Don't worry too much about damage to the chest — getting effective circulation is more important.) Then completely release the pressure. This cycle should be repeated about seventy times per minute. In very small dogs, you can achieve effective cardiac massage by applying pressure on the heart with one hand on each side of the chest wall or a single hand wrapped around the chest. If you are being effective you should be able to feel a pulse (see page 32) with each massage.

While attempts to restart the heart are being made, try to get the animal to a veterinarian. Don't expect the animal to revive during your attempts at resuscitation before obtaining veterinary services. If consciousness resumes, however, keep the dog warm and quiet and proceed to a veterinary hospital where observation can continue.

Convulsions

Convulsions (seizures) include a wide variety of signs consisting primarily of abnormal behavior and/or abnormal body movements. The most easily recognized signs are *loss* (or disturbance) *of consciousness, loss of motor control,* and *involuntary urination* and/or *defecation.* Convulsions fall into two main categories, in terms of whether or not they are emergencies:

1. The single convulsion which lasts for a minute or two and does not recur for at least twenty-four hours.

2. Repeated or continuous convulsions.

Convulsions in the second category require immediate veterinary attention. Dogs with convulsions in the first category should be examined by a veterinarian, but may not require emergency care.

The most important thing for you to do if your dog is having a convulsion is to provide gentle restraint so they won't injure themself. One of the best ways is to place a light blanket or towel over the dog. It's not a good idea to place your hand in or near the dog's mouth unless you are willing

Restrain a Dog Having A Convulsion

to risk a serious bite. Airway occlusion due to the tongue rarely occurs. While one person restrains the dog, another can try to reach a veterinarian. Seizures in the first category are often passed by the time you get in touch with a veterinarian.

Poisoning

Emergency situations involving convulsions occur commonly following poisonings. Snail bait *(metaldehyde or metaldehyde-arsenic)* and *strychinine* are the two poisons I see as the most frequent cause of convulsions.

Snail Bait Poisoning

Never put snail bait anywhere there is the slightest possibility that your dog may come in contact with it. There are snail bait holders designed to keep the bait away from pets. And, if necessary, you can resort to "old-fashioned" methods of snail and slug control, such as hand picking, the use of beer in a shallow container or a pet duck. Some snail baits contain metaldehyde alone (also found in compressed tablets for small heaters); other toxic ones contain arsenic as well as metaldehyde. (One type containing Mesurol® is claimed as non-toxic to dogs, but don't assume this about any garden product.) In cases of poisoning, even with the combination products, metaldehyde seems to be the toxic agent. First signs are uneasiness and muscle tremors which worsen until apparent convulsions occur. Vomiting may also be seen.

Induced Vomiting

If you see your dog eat snail bait, immediate induction of vomiting can prevent poisoning. The most reliable way to cause vomiting is to administer about a teaspoonful per five pounds body weight of *hydrogen peroxide* by mouth. If vomiting does not occur within five to ten minutes, you can repeat the dose at least two more times. A less effective way to cause vomiting is to place a teaspoonful of salt on the back of the dog's tongue. If signs of poisoning are already apparent when you first see the animal, DO NOT try to cause vomition, but rush your dog to a veterinarian. General anesthesia must usually be used for treatment.

Strychnine Poisoning

Strychnine is a potent poison often used in rodent and wild animal baits, and for malicious animal poisonings. The best way to protect your dog from strychnine poisoning is not to allow unsupervised roaming. Unsupervised dogs are more likely to come in contact with attractive baits set out

152

for pests or to become pests themselves, encouraging malicious poisonings.

The time of onset of signs of poisoning following the ingestion of strychnine varies depending on the fullness of the stomach and the form of the poison. Initially there may be restlessness and incoordination progressing to convulsions in which the legs are extended and the body rigid. A sudden stimulus such as a touch or noise will often initiate convulsions. At the onset of *any* signs indicative of poisoning contact your veterinarian. Intensive care including general anesthesia is usually necessary.

You can prevent poisoning from common household products by reading their labels carefully and using them appropriately. Any product labeled hazardous for humans should be assumed to be toxic for your dog as well.

General Treatment of Poisoning

1. If you see your dog ingest a toxic substance, induce vomiting unless the material is corrosive (strong acid, alkali or petroleum distillate e.g., kerosene.) Then give milk mixed with a raw egg at one fourth cup per ten pounds body weight.

2. If your dog gets a toxic substance on their skin, flush with large volumes of water while (or before) someone calls a veterinarian.

3. If convulsions occur try to restrain the dog.

4. Try to bring a sample of the suspected poison *in its original container* to the hospital.

Poison	Common Products Containing it	Immediate Treatment If Exposure Known	Signs which May Develop Following Exposure
Ethylene glycol	Antifreeze	Induce vomiting and rush to veterinarian	Immediate treatment necessary DO NOT wait for signs to appear
Organophosphate	Insecticides-coumaphos, dichlorvos, malathion, fenthion, ronnel	On skin: wash with alkaline detergent and wait for signs to appear	Salivation, small pupils, muscle tremors, vomiting diarrhea, inco-ordination, convulsions
Amphetamine	Diet and stimulant pills	Induce vomiting, wait for signs to appear	Mild cases: delirium, fever, dilated pupils. Severe cases: Convulsions, shock, coma
Arsenic	Ant poisons, herbicides, insecticides	If known ingestion, induce vomiting and consult veterinarian immediately. No home treatment effective.	Vomiting, restlessness, abdominal pain, diarrhea (sometimes bloody)
Thallium	Rodent poison	Consult veterinarian, no effective home remedy	Signs vary
Warfarin	Rodent poison	Consult veterinarian, no effective home remedy. Single dose may not cause signs	Hemorrhage-mainly internal. Pale mucous membranes, weakness
Alkali	Cleaning preparations, grease dissolvers, drain opener (sodium, potassium, ammonium hydroxide)	Externally: water and vinegar rinse Internally: vinegar by mouth	
Acids	Car batteries, some metal cleaners	Externally: flush with water, apply bicarbonate paste Internally: Magnesium hydroxide antacid, egg white, sodium bicarbonate	
Phosphorus	Strike anywhere matches (safety matches nontoxic), rat poisons, fireworks	Induce vomiting	Vomiting, diarrhea abdominal pain, collapse

The list of potentially dangerous garden and house plants is very long. The best rule to follow is to teach dogs to chew only on their own toys. Some of the more common poisonous plants are:

Plant	Poisonous Parts
Castor Bean	Seeds and foliage
Oleander	All parts
Monkshood	All parts
Autumn Crocus	All parts
English Ivy	Leaves, berries
Lily of the Valley	Leaves, flowers
Daphne	Bark, leaves, flowers
Larkspur	Young plants, seeds
Foxglove	Leaves
Golden Chain	Leaves, seeds
Daffodil	Bulbs

Dumbcane *(Diffenbachia)*, a common houseplant, causes irritation of the mouth, laryngitis and temporary paralysis of the vocal cords when eaten.

Snakebite

If your dog is bitten by a poisonous snake, prompt action by you and your veterinarian is necessary. Bites of poisonous snakes cause severe pain, so a bitten dog will often become excited and run. You should attempt to prevent this response, since exercise helps spread the venom. Immobilize the dog as soon as possible.

If the bite is on an extremity, apply a flat tourniquet between the body and the wound (nearest the wound). Unless the dog is very small, the tourniquet should be loose enough to barely slip one finger under, and it *should not* be fully loosened until the bite is treated by a veterinarian or until two hours have passed. (This type of application allows some oxygen to reach the tissues beyond the tourniquet.) If possible keep a bitten limb on a level horizontal with the heart. Then make linear incisions (not "X"-shaped) over the fang wounds and apply suction (preferably not by mouth but with a suction cup.) (For coral snake bites, *immediately* apply a tight tourniquet and *quickly* cut away a wide area of tissue surrounding and including the fang wounds.)

Get your dog to a veterinarian as soon as possible. The veterinarian will administer antivenin, antibiotics and pain relievers, and can administer other medical treatment as necessary. It may be necessary to remove a large portion of the wound surgically. Even if this is not done, snake bites often cause large portions of skin to die and slough, leaving a large wound that must be treated. Plan on your dog being hospitalized for a minimum of twenty-four to forty-eight hours. If you are traveling to a snake-infested area, discuss the possibility of your carrying a supply of antivenin with your veterinarian, and of, course get a good snakebite kit, boots and gloves.

Fishhooks In Skin

Fishhooks are foreign bodies which become embedded in dogs' skin relatively frequently. Once the barb has passed under the skin, a hook will not fall out on its own. The only way to remove it is to push the barb through the skin. Once through, cut the curved part of the hook just below **FISH HOOK** the barb and pull the rest of the hook back out through the original hole. Often this procedure is too painful to be done without Cut Here anesthesia so don't be surprised if you need the help of a veterinarian. Veterinary services are needed to administer antibiotics as well; unless the hook was *extremely* clean, this type of wound is likely to become infected.

Porcupine Quills In Skin

The important thing to remember about a porcupine quill in the skin is to remove the *whole* thing. Grasp the quill with a pair of pliers near the point where it disappears into the skin; then, with a quick tug, pull it out. If the quill breaks off as you try to remove it or if some of the quills have broken off before you had a chance to try and remove them, you may need a veterinarian's help. DO NOT ignore pieces of quill you cannot pull from the skin. They can migrate long distances (sometimes into bone) carrying sources of infection with them. And remember to check for quills inside the mouth as well as in the body surface.

Insect Bite or Sting

Owners usually become aware of insect bites or stings long after they have happened. Usually a large swelling of the muzzle is noticed with no particular evidence of pain. Other times hives *(wheals)* appear. These are allergic reactions to the bite or sting. If there is no fever and the dog acts normally (even though abnormal in appearance), no treatment is usually necessary, but pull out the stinger if you see it. Swelling should go away in about forty-eight hours. If you catch the bite early, or if signs are progressing (e.g., difficult breathing), consult a veterinarian. Corticosteroids may be administered to prevent signs or further progression of signs already apparent.

Burns

Burns may be thermal, chemical or electrical (electric shock). The severity of *thermal* (heat) burns in dogs may be underestimated because their appearance differs considerably from those in man. Blisters characteristic of superficial burns in humans may not form in the burned skin of a dog. Instead, the hair remains firmly attached in a superficial burn. If you pull on the hair in the area of a burn and it comes out easily, the burn is deeper and more serious.

Immediate treatment of thermal burns consists of applying cold water or ice compresses for twenty minutes. A soothing antibacterial medication can then be applied. Deep burns or burns covering large areas need emergency veterinary care. Because of the difficulty in evaluating the severity of burns in dog skin immediately after their occurence, it is a good idea to have all burns examined by a veterinarian within twenty-four hours of their occurence.

Thermal Burns

Electrical burns often occur in puppies who chew on electric cords. They can cause severe damage to the skin of the mouth and *pulmonary edema* (fluid in the lungs). Dogs sustaining such burns should be thoroughly examined by a veterinarian as soon as you become aware of the injury. If difficult breathing or cough occurs, pulmonary edema may be present. In severe cases the tongue and gums may look bluish. If you find your dog unconscious and not breathing

Electrical Burns (Electric Shock)

157

after electric shock, administer artificial respiration. (see page 149). If general signs do not develop after electric shock, mouth tissue damaged by the burn often dies and sloughs several days later and needs veterinary attention.

Chemical Burns

For information on chemical burns see *acids* and *alkali* in the chart of common household poisons, page 154.

Heat Stress (Heat Stroke)

Heat stress occurs most often in dogs that have been confined to a car (or other enclosure) with inadequate ventilation on a warm day. Temperatures inside a parked, poorly ventilated car can rapidly reach over one hundred degrees F on a relatively mild seventy-five to eighty degree day. Heat stress can also occur in dogs suddenly transported to a hot climate to which they have not been previously acclimatized. Puppies, *brachicephalic* (short-nosed) dogs, fat dogs and older dogs are more subject to heat stress than others.

Use Cold Water To Treat Heat Stress

Signs of heat stroke are panting, increased pulse rate, congested mucous membranes (reddened gums), *and an anxious or staring expression.* Vomiting is common. Stupor and coma may occur if the stress is allowed to continue long enough. Rectal temperatures are elevated (106 to 109 degrees F). Immediate treatment by immersion in cold water is necessary. If you cannot immerse the dog, spray them with cold water. Massage the skin and flex and extend the legs to return blood from the peripheral circulation. Then get your dog to a veterinary hospital where treatment can be continued.

Dogs sustaining heat stress should always be examined by a veterinarian, but if this is impossible, take their temperature frequently over a twenty-four hour period because elevation of the rectal temperature often recurs after the initial drop and first signs of improvement. It has been suggested that if the rectal temperature has not reached 103 degrees F in ten to fifteen minutes after starting treatment, a cold water enema should be given. Following this treatment, however, the rectal temperature is no longer accurate.

You Can Prevent Heat Stress

Prevent heat stroke by carrying water with you on hot days and by giving your dog small amounts frequently. Wet towels placed over your dog will provide cooling by

158

evaporation. Open car windows when a dog is left inside, or better yet, don't leave the dog in the car. And contrary to some opinions, clipping a long-haired dog is *not* an effective way to prevent heat stress.

Eclampsia (Puerperal Tetany, Milk Fever)

Eclampsia *(puerperal tetany)* usually occurs within two or three weeks after delivery although it can occur before delivery. Although the exact cause is unknown, it is due to a defect in calcium metabolism which results in an abnormally low blood calcium level. Heavily lactating females with large litters seem predisposed to the disease.

The first signs are often restlessness, whining and rapid breathing. Spontaneous recovery may result, or the signs may progress to stiffness, recumbency, convulsions and fever. *Progressive tetany is an emergency* which must be treated by a veterinarian. Calcium preparations are given intravenously. Puppies are removed from nursing for at least twenty-four hours. They may be returned to restricted nursing later, but this must be supplemented by hand feeding. Puppies old enough to eat solid food are weaned. Calcium-phosphorus-vitamin D supplements are often prescribed for mothers who must continue restricted nursing.

Certain females seem predisposed to milk fever and it may be advisable to not rebreed these females. A ration adequate in calcium, phosphorus and vitamin D should be fed throughout pregnancy. Some veterinarians, however, feel that oversupplementation may help induce milk fever. Therefore supplementation during pregnancy should be with balanced vitamin-mineral preparations used cautiously. Discuss this in detail with your veterinarian if your female is to be bred.

Geriatric Medicine
(Care as Your Dog Ages)

General Information

The life expectancy of the dog varies considerably between breeds and with the kind of health care received throughout their life. In general, large dogs age faster than small dogs. Giant breeds, such as Great Danes or Saint Bernards, are considered "old" at eight or nine years. Small breeds, such as the Chihuahua, often live until fifteen or sixteen.

Old Dogs May Not Adjust Well To Changes

In general the old dog is less adaptable to stress. Sudden changes in diet, routine or environment are probably best avoided if they have not been part of the dog's routine in the past. Many old dogs do not adapt well to hospitalization and therefore need special care when ill. Good veterinarians are aware of this and provide special attention or make special arrangements for the care of such older animals.

Geriatric Diet

Special diets need to be provided for old dogs with degenerative changes of the kidney and heart or other major organs. Many other times the addition of a balanced vitamin-mineral supplement to the normal diet is sufficient to meet any special needs imposed by the aging process. Since each dog is an individual, the need for special diet should be discussed with a veterinarian familiar with your aging dog.

Geriatric Exercise

Exercise should be continued as your dog ages to the degree the dog desires, unless a specific condition (e.g., heart disease) exists which requires that exercise be restricted. Again a veterinarian familiar with your dog can advise you best.

Some conditions which are likely to develop in dogs with age are covered in this section. Not all are disabling or progressive and most, if recognized early, can be treated at least palliatively. To use this section for diagnosing signs, refer to the Index of Signs on page 100, as well as to the General Index.

Lens Sclerosis

The formation of new fibers in the lens of the dog's eye continues throughout life. As new fibers are formed the older ones are compressed and pushed toward the center of the lens. This results in a continually increasing density of the lens. The lens also loses water as it ages, a factor contributing to increased density as well. This process is called *nuclear sclerosis* and should be recognized as a normal part of the aging of the dog's eye. It results in a bluish or greyish-white haze in the part of the lens which can be seen through the pupil. It *does not* normally interfere with vision and does not need treatment. This condition is often erroneously referred to as *cataracts* (lens opacities which interfere with light transmission to the retina.) In truth senile cataracts, which can cause loss of vision, occur much less commonly.

Cataracts

If your dog does develop cataracts as an aged (or sometimes young) dog and loss of vision occurs, there are surgical procedures which can be used to remove the opacity and restore vision. This surgery is not performed routinely because cataracts are relatively uncommon and most dogs adjust completely to a gradual loss of vision.

Deafness

Gradual loss of hearing occurs commonly as dogs age. The anatomical changes responsible for this loss are not well established and treatment is not possible. Inattentiveness or slowed response to commands is often one of the first signs of hearing loss. Unfortunately these signs are often mistakenly attributed to stubbornness and the dog is punished instead of accommodations being made for the hearing loss. A crude test for hearing ability is to stand behind the dog and make a sudden sound such as a whistle, hand clap or sharp call. Most dogs will cock their ears toward the sound or turn around. Hands clapped near the ear (but not near or in front of the eyes) may cause both eyes to blink in response to the sound.

Osteoarthritis (Arthritis)

Osteoarthritis is a joint disease in which the *cartilages* (fibrous caps) covering the articular surfaces of the

161

bones degenerate and bony proliferation (excess bone growth) occurs. This condition usually results in pain and lameness of the involved joints. It may occur in single joints of young dogs with congenital joint defects (e.g., *hip dysplasia*) or following any kind of joint trauma. When it occurs as an aging change it affects several joints, although lameness may not be apparent in all those affected. The lameness present with arthritis is often most severe on arising and improves with exercise. If you gently move the affected joints you may hear or feel *crepitus* (bone grating against bone). X-ray films will show the affected joints and the severity of bone changes. Although you may not become aware of the disease until signs occur, the changes characteristic of arthritis have usually been occuring over a long prior period.

There is no effective means of arresting the progression of osteoarthritis in older dogs, so treatment is usually symptomatic, directed at relieving any significant pain. Mild intermittant lameness or lameness that is only present on arising usually needs no treatment. Aspirin is the preferred pain reliever for more severe pain because of its lack of major side effects. Your veterinarian can prescribe corticosteroid or other anti-inflammatory drugs, if aspirin is not sufficient. Weight reduction often significantly improves lameness in obese dogs with osteoarthritis.

Tumors (Neoplasms, Cancer)

A *tumor* is an abnormal growth of tissue (*neoplasm* means new growth). *Benign tumors* are those which are likely to remain at the site of their original growth. *Malignant tumors* (cancer) are neoplastic growths which invade surrounding tissue and travel via blood vessels or lymph channels to other body sites where they start to grow anew. As dogs age the likelihood of a tumor occurring increases.

Many tumors occur internally where you would not likely be aware of them until they have grown quite large. You should, however, watch carefully for growths in the mouth and on the outside of your dog's body. On females it is wise to check each mammary gland periodically (e.g., once a month) for new growths. If you find a tumor in a young or old dog, it is always best to discuss its removal with a

162

veterinarian. If you don't feel that you can see a veterinarian, watch the tumor carefully for growth. If you notice growth be sure to investigate possibilities for removal. Some malignant tumors *metastasize* (spread) while the original tumor is still very small.

Old dogs are subject to the growth of tumors of the oil producing skin glands *(sebaceous adenomas)* in particular. These are usually small, lightcolored, hairless growths which look as if they are stuck on the skin. They are often described as wart-like or cauliflower-like. They are benign and do not usually need to be removed except for cosmetic reasons.

Sebaceous Adenomas

Heart Disease

There are several forms of heart disease in the older dog similar to those in people. The most common type is *valvular fibrosis* (chronic valvular fibrosis) in which the valves that separate each ventricle from its atrium (see page 31) become thickened and contracted so that they no longer form an adequate seal against the back flow of blood. This causes the heart to become progressively more inefficient as a blood pump until it is no longer able to supply the needs of the body tissue *(heart failure)*. It is important to understand that heart disease (of many types) can be present long before actual failure occurs. Heart disease generally progresses through several stages where it can be treated and the signs ameliorated before heart failure, requiring emergency treatment or resulting in death, occurs.

A *murmur* caused by abnormal turbulence of blood in a heart with "leaky valves" may be the first sign of heart disease in an older dog. Your veterinarian may mention a murmur's presence at the time of your dog's yearly physical exam and shots. Or you may hear a murmur as a "shhh" interposed between the normal lub-dup of the heart beat when you are examining your dog. If the murmur is intense enough you may even be able to feel it through the chest wall as the heart beats. The presence of a murmur in any age dog is not necessarily something to be alarmed about, but it is something that requires examination by a veterinarian. They may suggest chest x-rays, an electrocardiogram and other tests.

Heart Murmurs

In cases where you are unaware of a murmur, or a murmur is not present, you may first notice easy tiring with exercise or a low-pitched, deep cough. You may notice the cough more frequently in the morning or at night. Sometimes it will occur when the dog is excited and pulls on the leash, exercises, or drinks water. Mucus may be gagged up. If your older dog has any such signs, consult your veterinarian. If left untreated, heart disease progresses over a variable period of time to complete heart failure with severe difficulty in breathing, coughing even at rest, bluish-colored tongue and gums, rapid heart rate and inability to exercise.

Treatment of canine heart disease in the older dog is generally directed at improving circulatory function, since the aging process cannot be arrested. In the earliest stages no treatment is necessary. As your veterinarian follows the progression of the disease, they will ask you to feed your dog a low sodium diet (to help prevent fluid retention), which can either be purchased already prepared or made up at home. Medical treatment includes drugs which dilate the airways, *digitalis*-like drugs to increase the strength of heart contractions and *diuretics* to help control sodium and water retention that accompanies heart failure. With the help of a good veterinarian, treatment of heart disease in the older dog can be relatively easy. The benefits of keeping a close watch on an older dog's heart function can be substantial — including a longer, more comfortable and more active life.

Kidney Disease

Many older dogs have decreased kidney function due to aging changes and/or urinary tract disease processes which have gone undetected earlier in life. Because the kidneys have a large amount of tissue reserve, signs attributable to progressive kidney disease are often not apparent without laboratory tests until damage is severe and often irreversible.

Increased water drinking accompanied by increased volume of urination are often signs of kidney disease. As the kidneys degenerate, less functioning tissue is available to excrete the same amount of wastes produced by the body as when the kidneys were healthy. In an effort to maintain a normal physiological state, a larger volume of urine in which the wastes are less concentrated must be excreted and the

164

dog must drink more water daily. The need to excrete large volumes of urine will sometimes cause an old (or young) dog without free access to the outside to urinate in the house. This dog has not "forgotten their housetraining" or "grown senile," the volume of urine is just too great to be held for several hours. The only way to remedy this situation is to take the dog for walks more frequently or to provide free access to the yard. Restricting water will not help, but can actually make the dog sick since it interferes with waste excretion.

When the dog cannot compensate for failing kidneys, vomiting, lack of appetite and weight loss are other signs that may develop. If your dog has any signs of failing kidneys consult your veterinarian immediately. Other diseases (e.g., *diabetes mellitus*) may have similar signs and diagnosis requires laboratory tests including urinalysis and blood tests. Your veterinarian will try to find out if the disease process can be arrested and advise you on care which can prolong your dog's comfortable life in spite of diseased kidneys.

Euthanasia

It would be nice if all old pets which died did so peacefully in their sleep with no previous signs of illness. This doesn't always happen, though, and sometimes you must decide whether to end your dog's life or allow a progressive disease to continue. This is never an easy decision. A mutually close and trusting relationship with a veterinarian established when your dog is still young may help if you ever have to face this problem. A veterinarian familiar with your dog's medical history can tell you when a condition is irreversible and progressive and give you an opinion as to when that condition is truly a burden for your dog.

It is unfair to you, your pet and the veterinarian to take an animal to a new veterinarian and request euthanasia. A veterinarian not knowing your dog may perform euthanasia because you requested it when the condition was actually treatable. A veterinarian unfamiliar with you may refuse this heart-rending act because your dog seems healthy, not knowing that continuing to live with the dog is an extreme burden on you. Most veterinarians enter the profession to make animals well, not kill them. Too often I see people who react emotionally without knowing the facts, and insist that their pet be "put to sleep" for a condition which can be treated and with which their dog can live happily. In other cases euthansia is requested because a new pet is cheaper than treatment. The joy of life outweighs minor discomforts for most people, and I believe (perhaps too anthropomorphically) for most pets as well. The monetary value of a pet's life, I suppose, depends on each individual's philosophy. If you decide you just don't want a healthy animal any more, give it to a friend that does want it or take it to a shelter or pound where humane euthansia is performed.

When you and your veterinarian are in agreement about ending the life of a pet, you need not worry about discomfort. Euthanasia in veterinary hospitals is performed by the intravenous injection of an overdose of an anesthetic drug. Death is both rapid and painless.

Home Medical Care

Nursing at Home
Drug Information

Your Dog's Medical Record

Date	Temperature	Stool	Urine	Miscellaneous — include here medication, times given, times wounds cleaned, unusual signs, changes, etc.

Xerox this page to use for record keeping while nursing your pet at home.

Home Medical Care

Nursing at Home

The average dog has few illnesses for which they will have to be hospitalized during their lifetime. Most veterinarians are anxious to have your dog recuperate at home if they think you can provide adequate nursing. In some cases there are no alternatives to hospitalization, but when there are, when the sick animal can convalesce at home, there are several procedures you should be familiar with.

Record Keeping

If your dog has a serious illness, regular and accurate record keeping is invaluable in helping your veterinarian help you treat your dog at home. Take your dog's temperature at least once daily (preferably at the same time) and record the value. Record how much your dog eats and drinks, how often they urinate and the type of bowel movements they pass. An indication of the times and amounts of medication given is also helpful, as well as a record of any unusual signs (e.g., vomiting) or any other change in condition.

Temperature

Use a rectal thermometer to take your dog's temperature. An oral thermometer can be used in a pinch, but the bulb is more likely to break off. Before inserting the thermometer into the rectum, shake the mercury column down below ninety-nine degrees F and lubricate the tip of it with any non-toxic greasy substance (petroleum jelly, lubricant jelly, vegetable oil). Hold your dog's tail up with one hand and insert the thermometer into the rectum with a firm, gentle push. This is most easily done with the dog standing, but can be done while they sit or lie down. How far you need to insert the thermometer to get an accurate rectal temperature depends on the size of the dog — in small dogs an inch may be adequate, for large dogs it takes half the length of the thermometer or more. If you feel the thermometer go into a fecal mass when you insert it, try again. The thermometer should be left in two or three minutes, although many thermometers will register an accurate temperature in about one minute. (Helpful information if you have a squirmy dog!)

THERMOMETER

To read the thermometer, roll it back and forth between your fingers until you can see the thin mercury column inside. The point where the column stops is the temperature. Each large mark indicates one degree, each small mark two-tenths of a degree. Normal is usually between 101.0 and 102.5 degrees F.

Pulse, Heart Rate

For how to take your dog's pulse and measure the heart rate see page 31.

How to Pill Your Dog

The only way to be sure your dog has really swallowed medication in pill, capsule or tablet form is to administer it in the following way: Grasp your dog's muzzle with one hand and tilt their nose upward at about a forty-five

170

degree angle. Gently press inward on their upper lips; this usually causes the mouth to open at least slightly. Keep the upper lips rolled inward between the dog's teeth and your fingers; this keeps most friendly dogs from clamping their mouths completely closed on your fingers. If you have a large dog, insert your opposite, pill-containing fingers into their open mouth and place the pills as far back over the base of the tongue as possible. Quickly remove your hand, letting the dog close their mouth. Try to keep your dog's nose pointed upward during the whole procedure; it seems to encourage swallowing. If your dog licks their nose, you can be fairly certain they have swallowed the medication.

PILLING

If your dog is one of the smaller breeds, you will have to modify the procedure a little. Grasp the pill between your thumb and forefinger, and, as you use your third finger to hold their lower jaw open, place the pill over the base of the tongue. If your dog is extremely tiny or your fingers large, you will have to take aim and drop the pills over the back of the tongue instead of placing them there.

Most dogs are extremely easy to pill, particularly if you have been handling and examining them from a young age. If you do not get the pills in the center of the tongue or far enough back, your dog will spit them out and you'll have to start again. If the pills are not slippery enough or seem relatively large, buttering them may help you administer them. If you absolutely cannot get the pills down the way I've described, you can resort to wrapping them in a piece of cheese or meat. If your dog gulps their food, they will gulp the pill down easily. You can try crushing a tablet or emptying the contents of a capsule then mixing the drug thoroughly with a small portion of meat or some other favorite food. Most medications taste so bad that a sick dog will not take them this way. If it can be avoided, do not use these methods of administration. You can never be sure that your dog has taken all the medication when it is administered in food. If you grind an *enteric-coated* (coated to be absorbed by the intestine) tablet or empty the contents of a capsule into food, you may be preventing normal absorption from the gut. Coverings are often designed to remain intact until the drug reaches the part of the gut where it is best and most safely absorbed.

Liquid Medication (Force Feeding)

The simplest way to give your dog liquid medication is by placing it in the space between the outside surfaces of the

MEDICATING IN "CHEEK POUCH"

molar teeth and the inside surface of the cheek. If you place your finger into this area and pull the cheek slightly outward, you can pour liquids directly into it from a bottle or spoon. This works best if the dog's muzzle is tipped slightly upward and held in this position until your finger is removed and they have swallowed.

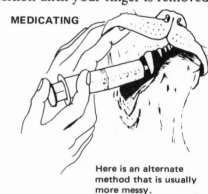

MEDICATING

A syringe, eyedropper or turkey baster can also be used to give liquid medication. Fill it and place it directly into the cheek space. Slowly administer the liquid as you hold the dog's muzzle steady

Here is an alternate method that is usually more messy.

allowing the dog to swallow as the liquid is given. Large quantities can be administered relatively easily with this method.

Force feeding is sometimes necessary when nursing a sick dog. Blended foods and water can be force fed in the same ways as liquid medication. Food balls can be given in the same manner as pills. Some special diets are indicated in this book; other times, if your dog needs special feeding, your veterinarian will recommend a specific diet.

Eye Medication

Ophthalmic ointments are most easily applied into the conjunctival sac (see page 19). Use your thumb or forefinger to roll the lower eyelid gently downward and squeeze the ointment into the space exposed. Eyedrops should be instilled with the dog's nose tilted slightly upward. Use one hand to grasp the dog's muzzle and hold the lower lid open. Rest the base of the hand holding the dropper bottle above the eye to hold the upper lid open, then drop in the medication. Avoid touching the end of the ointment tube or dropper bottle to the eye to prevent contamination of the solution and injury to the eye.

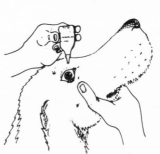

EYE DROPS

Ear Treatment

When your dog's ears become inflamed (see page 116) a more thorough cleaning than you give them routinely is often necessary. In most cases, inflamed ears should be examined and cleaned by a veterinarian who will have the necessary tools for visualizing the ear canal and ear drum during and after cleaning. Also, if the ears are painful, anesthesia is usually necessary to make most dogs hold still for a thorough and safe ear cleaning.

Cleaning Ears

Veterinarians use several methods for cleaning ears. In one method a rubber bulb syringe filled with a warm water-antiseptic soap solution or a wax-dissolving solution is inserted into the ear canal and used to flush the fluid in and out of the ear. This is done several times and is followed by clear water or antiseptic rinses. The clean ear canal is dried with cotton swabs and appropriate ear medication is instilled. Another method relies on cotton-tipped swabs and the use of an instrument called an *ear loop.*

173

If you cannot take your dog to a veterinarian and your dog is very cooperative, you may be able to use the bulb syringe method for ear cleaning. Use a warm solution, and flush the fluid in and out gently until all debris is removed. You can dry the vertical part of the canal with swabs, but it is probably not a good idea to try to dry the horizontal part without an otoscope. (If you are not familiar with the anatomy of the dog's ear turn to page 20).

Medicating Ears

After your dog's ears are cleaned you will usually have to instill medication in them at least daily for one to two weeks. Most ear ointments have long nozzles which are placed into the ear canal. Liquids can be dropped into the

canal. After the medicine is in the canal, grasp the lower part of the auricular cartilage through the skin and massage it up and down vigorously. If you are doing it properly, you will hear the medication squishing around inside. This will spread the medication down the length of the ear canal and is a very important part of nursing the ear properly.

I think it is a good idea to partially clean the ear daily while it is being medicated. One way is to use a cloth, as described in routine care of the ear page 49.

CLEANING AND MEDICATING THE EAR

Another, more effective, way is to use a cotton swab. Grasp the end of the pinna and hold it straight up over the dog's

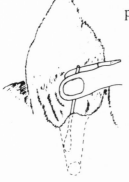

head. Insert the swab into the ear canal parallel to the side of the head. You cannot damage the eardrum if you keep the swab vertical and parallel to the side of the head. Use the swab to clean out old medication and debris before instilling the new. Turn the swab gently and try to lift out debris rather than compacting it.

Wounds and Bandages

Wounds which require repeated cleansing at home are infected traumatic wounds and abscesses (see page 107). These wounds are left open or partially open when treated to allow pus drainage and cleaning. A three per cent solution of *hydrogen peroxide,* which you can buy in drugstores, is suitable for use in such wounds.

Cleaning Open Wounds

Hydrogen peroxide is an unstable solution which decomposes to water and oxygen when it comes in contact with tissue. When it decomposes it has a transient and weak germicidal effect, and it forms bubbles which are effective in removing debris from infected wounds. If the opening of the wound is large enough, you can pour the solution directly into it. A bulb syringe or turkey baster can be used to flush the solution into smaller wounds. The hydrogen peroxide can be applied to a gauze pad which is used to wipe the wound or to a cotton-tipped swab which can be inserted into very small wounds. As the solution bubbles, it becomes warm. Some dogs find this uncomfortable. Clean the wound until visible tissue looks free of debris and/or the solution runs clear. Repeat the cleansing twice a day until debris no longer accumulates in the wound.

Wounds usually heal most rapidly when left uncovered. In cases where the wound is continually becoming contaminated or when the dog licks at the wound so much that they are preventing healing or making the wound worse, it must be protected.

A light bandage for a foot can be made by placing a sock over it and taping the sock to the leg with several wraps of adhesive tape applied to the top of the sock and leg. (Be sure the tape is loose enough to allow circulation to the foot.) This type of wrap leaves most of the sock loose and allows some air circulation. It is best for covering the nails to prevent damage when a dog is scratching at a wound or to protect areas of the foot from licking. Ointments can be applied under such bandages, and the sock will keep the medication on the foot and off the carpet.

SOCK BANDAGE

Bandaging Feet

175

A more substantial foot bandage is made using roll or tubular gauze and adhesive tape. Pad the areas between the toes with small pieces of cotton and cover the wound with a gauze or non-stick pad. Wrap the foot firmly with gauze, applying several layers vertically as well as around the foot. Follow the gauze with adhesive tape. The long vertical strips not only form the end of the bandage, but help prevent it from wearing through. Try to apply even pressure from the toes to the top of the bandage.

TAPE BANDAGE

Flexible wire or electrical tape may be wrapped over the bandage to help prevent your dog from chewing at it. Bandages should be changed at least every third day unless your veterinarian directs you differently.

Abdomen, Back and Neck Bandages

"MANY TAILED" BANDAGE

Many-tailed bandages can be made from any rectangular or square piece of clean cloth. These bandages are best used to try to prevent a dog from licking at a wound on the abdomen, back or neck (e.g., incision following surgery). Gauze or cotton padding may be placed between the wound and the bandage.

Ear Bandages

Small wounds on the ear are often difficult to get to heal because of head-shaking. In order to prevent ear damage due to head-shaking, the ear can be bandaged to the head. It can be placed over the head and held in position with a tube of nylon stocking or other stocking which is taped to the skin at both ends. (Cut a hole in the stocking to allow the other ear to hang through, if you don't want both ears held up on the head.) Or tape can be applied to the ear edges to hold the ear up over the head. Elastic tape is less likely to cause neck irritation, but regular adhesive tape can be used. If the tape seems too tight around the neck, a small cut made perpendicular to the long edge of the bandage under the chin will often relieve the irritation.

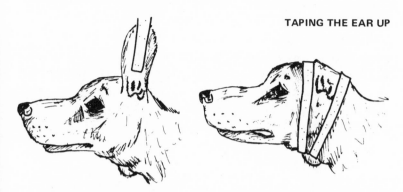

TAPING THE EAR UP

Some dogs will not leave wounds or other irritations alone no matter what bandaging method you try. They can prevent healing by continuing to lick at such areas. In these cases muzzles, elizabethan collars, or other means must be employed.

An appropriate muzzle can be purchased at a pet shop. *Wire Muzzles* Be sure the wire grid is small enough that your dog can't lick or chew through it.

Ready-made plastic or cardboard elizabethan collars can *Elizabethan* be purchased at some pet stores or from some veterinarians. *Collars*

CARDBOARD ELIZABETHAN COLLAR   **PLASTIC BUCKET**

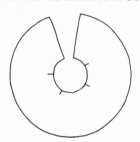

Or you can make one from heavy cardboard. An alternative to an elizabethan collar is a plastic wastebasket or bucket. Cut a hole in the bottom just large enough to slip the dog's

177

head through. The cut edges can be covered with adhesive tape to make them more comfortable.

Both the elizabethan collar and the bucket will prevent most dogs from disturbing wounds on their bodies. They are also effective against scratching of head wounds. However, some dogs cannot or will not eat or drink wearing an elizabethan collar. Be sure you allow for this. Also be sure you know the cause of their illness. A collar will prevent your dog from scratching at their ears, for example, but if they have *otitis* it won't cure the problem.

Making a Muzzle

It is extremely important to know how to apply an effective muzzle when dealing with an uncooperative dog. A muzzle does not hurt the dog or interfere with their breathing since dog noses are bony and the nasal passages cannot be compressed. A muzzle is for your protection and the protection of anyone helping you.

MUZZLE

Use a long strip of rope, heavy cord, gauze bandage or handkerchief. Form a loop and slip it over the dog's nose as far as possible. Draw the loop tightly around the nose, then bring the ends under the chin and tie them tightly again. Now bring an end along each side of the dog's head and tie them together firmly at the nape of the neck. If the muzzle is properly applied, the dog's biting efforts will be ineffective. A single loop tied under the chin may be used, but is much less effective than the double loop type.

178

Drug Information

General Information About Drugs

Drugs are identified by their formal *chemical name*, their *generic* name, and their *brand* (proprietary) *name*. The generic name is usually simpler and easier to remember than the formal chemical name. For example, *acetylsalicylic acid* is the formal chemical name for the drug generically called *aspirin*. If your veterinarian needs to write a prescription, request that they use the generic drug name rather than the brand name, if possible. This allows the pharmacist to give you the same drug usually for less money than the brand name drug would cost.

In general, veterinary drugs are the same as human drugs but less expensive when they are sold under a veterinary name. Many veterinarians dispense the drugs you need instead of writing prescriptions for you to take to a pharmacy. Although veterinary hospitals make a profit with this practice, for the most part it is a convenience for you and usually is less expensive than purchasing the equivalent medicine at a drugstore. Some companies sell drugs directly to people who are not veterinarians. In some cases the drugs are the same ones veterinarians use. In other cases, however, they are less effective or more likely to be toxic than the drugs a veterinarian would choose. I believe that companies which sell many of these drugs to laymen are interested primarily in profit, not animal health. They usually make few attempts to be sure the drugs are used properly and sometimes fail to warn of possible side effects. Try to avoid such drugs unless recommended by a veterinarian you trust.

All drugs dispensed by a pharmacist or veterinarian should be labeled with the generic or brand name, expiration date, concentration, and clear directions for use. This avoids misunderstandings in treatment and helps others who may treat the case later. Since drugs are helpers, not magic potions, your veterinarian should not be secretive about what is being dispensed. Keep in mind that drugs are changing all the time. Although I've mentioned some generic drugs in this book, better drugs may become available for use before this book is revised, so keep this in mind.

Antibiotics

Technically, *antibiotics* are chemical substances produced by microscopic organisms that interfere with the growth of other micro-organisms. In practice, antibiotics include a large number of substances, many man-made, which are used primarily in the treatment of bacterial infections. Antibiotics are miracle drugs when properly used. They enable us to cure infections that, in the past, would have certainly been fatal. They can, however, be easily misused.

All antibiotics are not effective against all bacteria. A veterinarian's decision to use a particular antibiotic is based on the probable bacteria causing the disease and/or the results of laboratory tests in which the infective organisms are grown and tested for antibiotic sensitivity. If the wrong antibiotic is chosen, there is no beneficial effect. If the proper antibiotic is chosen and given at the correct dosage, growth of the bacteria is stopped or at least controlled sufficiently that the body's own natural defense systems can overcome the infection. If you fail to give the antibiotic as frequently as prescribed or if you discontinue the medication too soon, forms of bacteria resistant to the antibiotic may develop, or the infection may recur.

Antibiotics are not always effective alone. Other drugs and special nursing techniques are often combined with their use. In cases of localized infection, such as abscesses, antibiotic treatment must often be used with proper surgical intervention for success.

Antibiotics Not Effective Against Viruses

Many people seem to believe that antibiotics are useful in any infectious or febrile disease. This is certainly untrue. A particularly common case where antibiotics may be of no help is the viral infection. *Viruses* exist in body cells and depend on their metabolic processes for reproduction. Since the methods of viral metabolism are unlike those of bacteria which for the most part survive outside of cells and multiply independently, drugs effective against bacteria are ineffective against viruses. When antibiotics are prescribed for use during viral infection, it is to combat bacteria which invade after the virus has weakened the animal *(secondary infection)*. There are very few drugs available for treatment of viral infections. Since viral reproduction is so intimately tied in with normal cellular function, most drugs found effective against viruses

180

also destroy body cells.

Like other drugs, most antibiotics have potential side effects. Since bacteria are single-celled organisms similar in many ways to the individual body cells, antibiotics can sometimes act against body cells in ways similar to the ways they adversely affect bacteria. Among the possible side effects are allergic reactions, toxic effects, alteration of metabolism, and alteration of normal (and beneficial) bacteria inhabiting the body. A good veterinarian will tell you if there are any side effects you should watch for when antibiotics are prescribed. Side effects can be potentiated by the use of outdated drugs, combining antibiotics with certain other drugs, and by certain illnesses.

Indiscriminate use of antibiotics is to be avoided. Use with proper guidance will avoid toxic effects and stem the development of antibiotic-resistant bacteria. Be glad, not disappointed, if your veterinarian feels that the condition can be treated without antibiotics and sends you away empty-handed. And don't use "leftover" antibiotics unless directed to by your veterinarian. Antibiotics are available over-the-counter as ointments for *topical* (on the body surface) use. Common effective ones contain *bacitracin, neomycin* and/or *polymixin B.* These are suitable to instill into wounds.

Adrenocortical Steroids

Adrenocortical steroids (corticosteroids) include hormones produced by the adrenal glands and synthetic drugs similar to these natural substances. This group of drugs has a wide range of actions on the body, among them effects on fat, protein, and carbohydrate metabolism, water balance, salt balance, and cardiovascular and kidney function. They are very important in the individual's ability to resist certain environmental changes and noxious stimuli.

Steroid drugs are commonly used in veterinary medicine for their effects against inflammation. (For example, to give relief from itching due to allergies or other skin diseases.) Because of the remarkable response following administration, some dog owners and some veterinarians are often inclined to misuse these drugs. Keep in mind that steroid drugs are only palliative, relieving but not curing disease, unless the condition is caused by deficiency of adrenal gland function.

181

Also keep in mind the fact that steroids are not without side effects. Although they are safe, even lifesaving, used properly, misused they constitute a threat to your dog's health. Avoid preparations containing steroids sold in pet stores and rely on the advice of a good veterinarian regarding the use of steroids in maintaining the health of your dog. Some names of common steroid drugs are *prednisone, prednisolone, cortisone, triamcinolone* and *dexamethasone.* Some have less wide-ranging effects than others.

Drugs You Might Have Around The House

Tranquilizers

Tranquilizers are drugs which work on the brain in several different ways to achieve desirable behavior in dogs. Even with the best-trained dogs, however, tranquilizers have legitimate uses in relieving anxiety and producing sedation. (Some also affect the brain's "vomiting center" reducing nausea induced by motion. See page 132). Veterinarians use tranquilizers to relieve anxiety which makes some dogs uncooperative when they enter veterinary hospitals. Other common reasons for tranquilizing dogs include prolonged confinement (as when traveling), noisy situations (e.g., Fourth of July, thunderstorms), and sedation to prevent self-trauma (as in wound licking).

If you can anticipate the need for tranquilization, it is best to discuss the pros and cons with your veterinarian and get a prescription for tranquilizing drugs from them. If an unanticipated need arises, two human tranquilizers which are used for dogs are *diazepam* (Vallium®) and *chlorpromazine* (Thorazine®). In such situations call your veterinarian and ask about the advisability of using the drug you have, and ask what the correct dose for your dog should be. Over-the-counter pet tranquilizers contain *antihistamines* (such as *methapyrilene*) and other drugs (e.g., *scopalamine*) which produce sedation normally thought of as a side effect of their medical use. In high doses the drugs may produce excitement, and I do not recommend their routine use. DO NOT use tranquilizers merely for your convenience; attempt to deal with recurrent problems by training. DO NOT use tranquilizers to sedate your dog following trauma which can produce severe injury (e.g., hit by a car); they can have an undesirable effect on blood pressure in such situations and

182

may contribute to shock.

Aspirin (acetylsalicylic acid) is a common household
drug occasionally useful in treating dogs. It relieves fever,
mild pain and has some anti-inflammatory effects, but is not
a specific cure for any disease. Aspirin relieves fever by acting
on the brain to reset the body's "thermostat." The way it
brings about its other effects is not known.

Aspirin

Aspirin should be used to relieve fever in dogs only if
the fever itself is high enough (106 degrees F) and prolonged
enough to possibly be damaging in itself. This rarely occurs.
In many other cases of fever it simply masks the signs and
makes diagnosis more difficult. Aspirin's best use is probably
to relieve pain associated with osteoarthritis in dogs. Of all
the drugs available for relief of pain and inflammation
associated with this condition, aspirin is the safest. Although
aspirin is generally safe, it is irritant to dogs' stomachs and
can cause vomiting and stomach ulcers. Use it only when
necessary to relieve signs not treatable in other ways. Give
aspirin at the rate of five grains per thirty-five pounds body
weight no oftener than every six hours.

The use of antacids is discussed on pages 131 and 132.

Antacids

The use of antidiarrheal drugs (intestinal protectants) is
discussed on page 133.

Antidiarrheals

The use of drugs with laxative action is discussed on
page 134.

Laxatives

See page 175 for how to use hydrogen peroxide to
clean wounds. To use it to induce vomiting see page 152.

Hydrogen peroxide

You can try isopropyl alcohol for treatment of
inflamed ears; see page 117.

Isopropyl alcohol

Breeding and Reproduction

Breeding and Reproduction

General Information

Male and female *(bitches)* dogs usually reach puberty between six and twelve months of age. The actual onset of sexual maturity and the time of first breeding vary greatly with the individual dog because they are influenced by many factors; among them climate, nutrition, breed and psychological maturity. Small breeds are usually capable of reproduction before one year; large or giant breeds often are not. A male dog may be able to produce sperm and copulate normally as early as four or five months of age, but the actual time breeding first occurs is dependent on many social factors not associated with physical maturity. A dog low in the social order may not have the "confidence" necessary to breed successfully.

Bitches undergo a cyclical physiological rhythm of reproductive function called the *estrous cycle.* Each bitch has her own normal cycle which, once established, tends to repeat itself. Most breeds, however, show signs of heat approximately every six months. The basenji breed is an exception, ovulating only once a year, as is the case with many wild canids.

The bitch's reproductive cycle is divided into four stages: *anestrus, proestrus, estrus,* and *metestrus.* Understanding the estrous cycle is as important to those who want to breed their dog as it is to those who don't.

During *anestrus* the ovaries are quiescent. This period lasts about two to three months. The anestrus state can be artificially induced by the *ovariohysterectomy* or "spaying" operation (see page 189).

187

Proestrus is the time during which a bloody discharge first appears at the vulva of the female. Many people commonly consider this the beginning of "heat." During this stage the follicles from which the ova are produced are growing. Proestrus usually lasts about nine days; its end is marked by the female's first acceptance of the male.

Estrus is the period during which the bitch is sexually receptive and breeding can occur. Many females continue the bleeding, characteristic of proestrus, throughout all or part of estrus. In these cases there is no external physical indicator of the onset of estrus, except the sexual receptivity of the bitch. In other females bleeding stops when estrus begins. Ovulation usually occurs about twenty-four hours after the first acceptance of the male (about ten to eleven days after the onset of bleeding). Ova survive and are capable of being fertilized for at least four days following ovulation. Estrus lasts seven to nine days, or even longer in some females.

Metestrus follows estrus. It is characterized by a physiologic state of "pseudopregnancy" (see page 197), which is followed by a return of the uterus and ovaries to the anestrus, resting state.

Preventing Pregnancy

Because the estrous cycle shows so much individual variation, to prevent pregnancy in the unspayed female you must be constantly alert from the onset of bleeding (proestrus) until the end of receptivity (estrus), usually a total of about three weeks. Swelling of the vulva precedes the onset of heat often by as long as a month and sometimes longer. This can be used as a signal for the onset of heat, and is particularly helpful if your bitch does not bleed heavily. DO NOT let your female dog out of sight during heat unless she is confined in a dog-proof shelter. Dogs can perform remarkable feats to reach a female in heat. Even chain link fences have been

ANESTRUS   ESTRUS

VULVA

Vaginal Opening

Clitoris

scaled, dug beneath and torn down. Females who have gotten out of their owner's sight for only two or three minutes have been found "tied" with males. You must be *absolutely* sure your bitch is non-receptive before you allow her to associate with males. At the end of estrus a female will be aggressive to males, but a persistent dog will often be rewarded by final acceptance.

At this time there are no pills proven safe and effective for long term birth control in dogs available in the U.S. *Chlorophyll tablets*, which you can purchase from your veterinarian or a pet store, may help mask the attractive scent of the urine of a female in estrus, but are not an effective birth control method. In the past a progesterone-like compound, "Promone®," was used by veterinarians to prevent estrus. Its use, however, was found to be related to the occurrence of uterine infection several years after the drug's administration and has been discontinued.

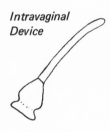

Several companies are working on products to prevent pregnancy. One method of birth control just recently marketed is a plastic *intra-vaginal device*, that can be placed in the female's vagina by a veterinarian. It works by preventing intromission. It shows promise as an effective method of birth control for owners who think they would like to allow their bitch to become pregnant at a later date or for people who feel they cannot afford an ovario-hysterectomy.

The best method currently available for permanently preventing pregnancy is the *ovariohysterectomy* or spaying operation. Many misconceptions surround this operation. One of the most prevalent is that the spay will cause a female to become fat and lazy. Not so. As stated earlier, this surgery induces a permanent state comparable to the natural anestrus. Dogs of either sex become fat only if they are using less calories than they are eating. Laziness usually accompanies excess weight. Fatness is sometimes caused by a metabolic abnormality (e.g., hypothyroidism), but it is sually caused by *overfeeding*, and it is not caused by spaying. I cannot tell a spayed female from an unspayed one when a fat dog waddles through the door. Many bitches are spayed when they are young. Owners forget that all dogs need less food as they age, but seem to remember when their dog is overweight that she was spayed and associate the two. Although some breeds tend to remain extremely active as they age, most dogs mature into more quiet adults. I think many people attribute this natural maturation to the spay, since the surgery is often performed before the female has formed her adult personality.

The best time to perform the ovariohysterectomy is before the first heat but not earlier than five to six months of age. The surgery is easiest to perform at this time (therefore easier on the dog), and females which are spayed before their first heat have a lower incidence of mammary tumors (breast cancer) than females spayed later. Some people (not most veterinarians) feel that it is better for a bitch to go through her first heat before spaying. In my experience, the heat has no beneficial effect. A female may act different during heat, while pregnant and while nursing, but, once the puppies are gone, most return to their usual anestrous personalities.

In most good veterinary hospitals the procedure for an ovariohysterectomy is similar to the following:

Veterinarians request that you withold food from your dog at least eight to twelve hours preceding surgery. This allows time for the stomach to empty preventing vomiting and aspiration of the vomitus into the trachea and lungs during general anesthesia. Preanesthetic drugs are given to reduce apprehension before surgery and to prepare the body for general anesthesia. Anesthesia is usually induced with a short-acting barbiturate drug given intravenously. Its effects

GAS ANESTHESIA

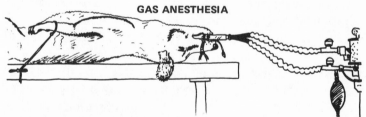

last just long enough to allow the veterinary surgeon to place an *endotracheal tube* into the dog's windpipe *(trachea)*. This airway is the path via which gas anesthetic agents and oxygen are administered to maintain sleep during surgery; it also provides a ready means for resuscitation if an emergency were to arise.

After the dog is sleeping, the abdomen is clipped free of hair, washed with surgical soap and disinfected. The dog is then transferred to the surgery area and placed on the operating table belly up. An  **ENDOTRACHEAL TUBE** assistant stands by to monitor anesthesia, breathing and heart function. The veterinarian, who has been scrubbing their hands and donning sterile clothing and gloves while the dog is prepared for surgery, steps in and places a sterile drape over the patient before surgery begins.

An incision into the abdomen is made at the midline. The length of the incision varies with the size of the dog and the difficulty of the surgery, but is usually one to four inches long. Most veterinarians use a special hook-like instrument to reach into the abdomen and pick up one horn of the uterus as it lies along the body wall. The uterine horn is brought out through the incision and followed to the ovary. Clamps are applied and the blood supply to the ovary interrupted by *ligatures* (ties around blood vessels) or metal vascular clips. The ovary is cut away from its blood supply, which is allowed to return to the abdomen. The other uterine horn and ovary are brought to the incision and treated in the same manner. Then the uterine horns are followed to their point of attachment to the body of the uterus. Its blood supply is interrupted by ligatures or clips and the uterine body itself is ligated. A freeing incision is made through the uterus, and the horns and ovaries are removed. (Turn to Anatomy page 29 if you need to review the structure of the uterus and ovaries.) The inner part of the incision is closed with layers of absorbable suture material or stainless steel; then the skin is *sutured* (stitched) closed. With modern anesthesia the dog begins to wake up shortly following the last stitches and is ready to go back to a kennel for final recovery. Most healthy dogs are completely themselves one or two days following surgery. In fact, most are feeling so good that it is often a chore to try to restrict their exercise.

When you take your female home following the surgery, it's a good idea to take her temperature and examine the incision daily even if you are not given specific instructions to do so by your veterinarian. (Good things to do following any surgery.) Fever and/or swelling, redness or discharge at the incision site should alert you to call your veterinarian for advice. Normal feeding should resume forty-eight hours following surgery. Many veterinarians allow you to take your dog home before this time; so if you do, provide small meals and water frequently but in small amounts at one time to avoid gastric irritation. Vomiting which occurs more than once or twice, especially if accompanied by inactivity, should again prompt you to call the hospital where the surgery was performed for advice.

*Tubal
Ligation*   Some veterinarians and spay clinics perform *tubal ligations* (tying of the fallopian tubes so the ova cannot pass into the uterus). This involves the same type of abdominal entry as an ovariohysterectomy and, although it is effective in preventing pregnancy, I think it has definite disadvantages when compared to an ovariohysterectomy. It does not prevent *pyometra* (see page 143) or influence the development of mammary tumors. It does not prevent signs of heat. If you are *sure* you won't mind the signs associated with a female dog in heat — bloody drips, attracting males — then you may choose a tubal ligation or better in terms of health, a *hysterectomy* (removes the uterus but leaves one or both ovaries). Remember, however, that neither prevents the signs of heat or has an effect on the incidence of mammary tumors. I know several people who chose a hysterectomy (or tubal ligation) only to change their minds a year or two later and request additional surgery to remove the ovaries.

Accidental Breeding

If your dog was bred accidentally, there are alternatives to having an unwanted litter. If you were planning to have your bitch spayed, your veterinarian can usually go ahead with the surgery. Particularly in the early stages, the surgery is not much more difficult than for a female in heat and the fee may be the same. In the later stages of pregnancy the surgery becomes more difficult and the fee increases accordingly.

If you have not yet decided on the question of spaying and if you can get your dog to a veterinarian soon after breeding (ideally within the first twenty-four hours), an injection of an estrogen-like compound followed by oral

192

medication given at home can be used to prevent pregnancy. Compounds used work by preventing implantation of the fertilized ova into their "beds" in the uterine wall. The signs of heat are prolonged following administration of these drugs, but no significant undesirable effects are common.

An actual abortion can be performed late in pregnancy if absolutely necessary. Methods similar to those used in humans have not generally been applied to dogs. Abortions in dogs, therefore, consist of *caesarian sections* in which the puppies are removed through uterine and abdominal incisions. This procedure usually results in blood loss, is stressful on the females and is not encouraged by most veterinarians.

Male Birth Control

Castration is the surgical removal of the testes. A *vasectomy* is the surgical removal of a portion of the vas deferens (see page 27) which conducts the sperm from the testes to the urethra. Both of these operations will prevent a male dog from impregnating a female. They are, however, inefficient methods of dog population control. If you live in an area where your male dog can roam unsupervised, a vasectomy (which has no effect on the ability or desire to breed) would be a good idea to prevent him from fathering unwanted litters.

Castration is usually employed as a means of modifying undesirable behavior in male dogs such as urinating in the house and excessive aggression. Prepubertal castration prevents the development of sexual responsiveness in the male dog. Castration after puberty usually reduces aggressive behavior and sexual responsiveness. Some males, however, will continue to breed (but not impregnate) following castration, and some continue undesirable scent-marking behavior.

Cryptorchidism

A *cryptorchid* dog has only one *(monorchid)* or no testicles descended into the scrotum. Males with this condition should not be allowed to breed because the defect is inherited, probably as a genetic recessive. If both testes have not descended by six to eight months of age, you should assume that the condition is permanent. It is believed that retained testicles are more subject to tumor formation than normal ones, therefore it is advisable to have retained testicles removed. If the defect is unilateral (monorchid), a vasectomy should be performed on the remaining teste to insure that the defect will not be passed on.

Breeding

Deciding to Breed

Before you decide to breed your dog ask yourself several questions. The first is are you sure you will find good homes for the puppies? Even with purebred dogs, permanent good homes are difficult to find. There is an extraordinary excess of dogs (and cats) in this country. In California alone in 1973 nearly *400,000* dogs were destroyed.* It is estimated that eighty to eight-five percent of all animals entering animal shelters and pounds are killed.* These are not just dogs that have strayed from home, but many are pets which have been taken to the pound by owners who know that they will almost certainly be destroyed. They are unwanted gifts, cute Christmas puppies who because they have grown into adults have lost their cuddly charm, dogs bought on impulse from a pet shop window, unmanageable dogs who became so because no one took the time to train them properly, and others both purebred and mixed. If you are not *sure* that your puppies won't end up in a pound or pet shop, and if you are not willing to provide a good home for puppies you can't find other homes for, do not allow your dog to breed.

Do you have a good place to keep the puppies and are you willing to care for them if the mother can't? Puppies aren't much trouble at all as long as their mother is taking care of them. If the female refuses to care for them or is unable to care for them, however, then you must assume the responsibility. Also, at about four weeks of age, when the puppies begin to eat solid food and can get around more easily, puppy rearing becomes more difficult. At this time the mother stops consuming the puppies' excreta and they are too young to housebreak, so you must be able to provide an

*1973, California Animal Control Survey, California Humane Council, 4432 Canoga Avenue, Woodland Hills, California 91364

194

adequate area in which to confine them when you can't be around picking up after them. This is one good reason to try to raise puppies in the spring and summer when, at least part of the time, confinement may be outside.

Why do you want to breed your dog? Almost everyone is awed by birth, and hardly anyone can resist the cuteness of a puppy, but the dog population cannot afford another litter bred solely so "the kids" or you can watch the birth. If this is the only reason for breeding, it might be better to make arrangements with a dairy, horse farm, or established kennel to watch a birth or to take advantage of films and books available on animal reproduction. If you are breeding for profit, you will find that it can be a fulltime business to produce *quality* purebred dogs at a profit. Many purebred breeders have dogs as a hobby because they know they are likely only to break even or take a loss. If you are breeding so the female can "have the experience of being a mother," I think you are being too anthropomorphic. I don't think dogs can anticipate the experience of having puppies and many (particularly those closely attached to humans) seem to prefer to neglect their puppies to be with their owners. Until the dog population reaches a more manageable size, our "best friends" will continue to experience mistreatment and neglect. Everyone, purebred breeders and pet owners alike, should think seriously before deciding to let their male or female breed and produce even a single litter.

If you decide that it is reasonable to breed your dog, *Before Breeding* you need additional information. Before a female is bred she should be vaccinated against distemper, hepatitis, leptospirosis and rabies (see page 65). Live vaccines should not be given during pregnancy, but the female should be fully protected before breeding so she can pass on a protective level of antibodies to her puppies in the *colostrum* (first milk). Have a fecal sample examined by a veterinarian to be sure a female to be bred is free from intestinal parasites which compete for nutrients. It is best to avoid breeding most bitches on the first heat unless they are definitely full grown. By waiting until the second heat, she won't have to try to get enough nutrients to meet both growth requirements and those of pregnancy. No special feeding is necessary before breeding, assuming your dog is already on a balanced diet, but avoid breeding obese females because they will have more difficulties at delivery. If your dog is over five years old at the time you first consider breeding, definitely consider preventing pregnancy. The incidence of difficult births is much higher in dogs first whelping after five.

*Breeding
Procedures* The ideal way to breed a female in order to insure maximum litter size is to take her to the male's home and allow her to remain there during the whole estrous period — letting breeding occur at will. Emotional factors play an important part in determining whether or not a male dog breeds — a dog may not breed in unfamiliar surroundings, or if he is fearful. Social factors also play a role; if the female does not "care for" the male, breeding often will not occur. If the male cannot be mated frequently with the female during estrus, then breeding should be allowed twenty-four hours after the female first shows signs of estrus and, if possible, again forty-eight hours later.

*Signs of
Estrus* Female dogs in estrus often urinate more frequently than usual and may assume a partial leg lifting posture. In the presence of a male, a normal female in true estrus will stand staunchly and wave her tail to one side to allow breeding to occur. You may also see vertical lifting of the vulva *(winking or tipping)* in response to the presence of the male. If you don't have a male "teaser" dog you can count the days from the beginning of bleeding and try breeding first on day ten or eleven, then every forty-eight hours afterwards until two successful matings have occured. This is probably the least reliable method. Your veterinarian can help you by examining a series of vaginal smears to give you an indication of when the female ovulates.

*Breeding
Behavior* Play will often precede the time a female allows herself to be bred. The actual copulation may last five to thirty minutes, or slightly longer. The male mounts the female from behind, clasping her around the loin with his forepaws. During a series of rapid pelvic thrusts intromission occurs; then the thrusts slow and a

MOUNTED

196

sperm-dense fluid is ejaculated. Engorgement of the bulbis glandis usually prevents the male from separating from the female at this time, which is called the *copulatory lock* or *tie.*

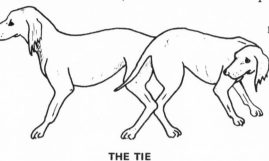

THE TIE

During the tie the male will often rest on the hindquarters of the female or turn around so that the dogs are rump to rump. The tie is not necessary for fertilization to occur since sperm are ejaculated early in coition. Do not try to separate dogs found tied — it is painful for both male and female, and will not prevent fertilization. Sperm survive about thirty hours in the female. Because ova survive about four days following ovulation, litters with several fathers are possible in dogs. So keep the female away from unwanted fathers after the breeding.

Determining Pregnancy

Between about three to five weeks following conception it is often possible for a veterinarian to palpate (feel) the fetuses in the uterus through the abdominal wall. At this time they are distinct lumps in the uterus. Later it is often impossible to feel the pups. An x-ray film taken after about six and one-half weeks of pregnancy (when the pups' bones are ossified) can be used for confirmation of pregnancy if palpation has failed. It is easy for a person unfamiliar with the reproductive cycle of the dog to think a dog is pregnant following estrus. Many dogs have an intensification of normal hormonal changes following estrus which results in a greater or lesser degree of false pregnancy *(pseudopregnancy).*

False pregnancy is characterized by deposition of abdominal fat, by mammary gland development and by milk flow in varying degrees, which occurs about fifty to seventy days following estrus. Some dogs make a nest and go through a pseudo-labor. Some show a mothering instinct by adopting toys or other objects, and some are even capable of nursing puppies. Pseudopregnancy seems to occur most

False Pregnancy

frequently and intensely in females that have been bred. Estrogen hormones and/or testosterone can be administered by your veterinarian to relieve signs of severe pseudopregnancy. However, I think it is best to avoid hormone treatment if possible. Females becoming pseudopregnant once tend to have false pregnancies each time they come in heat. An ovariohysterectomy is indicated to prevent recurrent signs.

Care During Pregnancy

Pregnancy normally lasts fifty-eight to sixty-eight days. Most bitches whelp around sixty-three days. Pregnancy increases the protein and calorie requirements of the mother, but no changes in caloric intake are necessary during the first four weeks. Throughout pregnancy it is extremely important not to overfeed and/or underexercise, to prevent obesity and poor muscle tone which can cause a difficult delivery. High quality proteins such as milk products, eggs and muscle meat should be used to improve the protein quality of your dog's regular diet. During the first four weeks such proteins can be substituted for part of the normal diet so the total caloric intake is not increased. Later in pregnancy, as total calorie requirements increase, they can be used in addition to the regular diet. Commercial high protein or puppy rations are also suitable for use during the last weeks of pregnancy and during lactation. Although food intake increases, calorie requirements on a *per pound* basis increase only slightly during pregnancy — to about fifty to sixty-five calories per pound per day — because the mother is gaining weight (due to growth of the fetuses) as her food intake increases. Increase the number of feedings per day as pregnancy progresses and continue multiple feedings throughout lactation. It is often impossible for a bitch to take in all the necessary food in one or two meals, particularly as the uterus enlarges and begins to compress the other abdominal organs. You can allow your female to self-feed as long as she is not becoming too fat. If you are using a high quality commercial ration as a basic diet, vitamin-mineral supplements are not necessary during pregnancy. If you are concerned about possible deficiencies, talk to a veterinarian who can supply you with a balanced vitamin-mineral supplement.

Most dogs restrict their exercise sufficiently as the time of delivery approaches. The last few days before delivery, however, be sure not to encourage strenuous exercise (e.g., long hikes).

To minimize psychological stress, accustom your dog to a warm and draft free whelping area well before the time of delivery. If you have provided your dog with a sleeping area from the time she was a puppy, there shouldn't be any trouble getting her adjusted to the whelping area. A whelping box should have sides high enough to keep the puppies from falling out, but low enough that the mother can get in and out easily (three to six inches). If you like, you can provide a completely enclosed whelping box with a door opening and removable top, but this is not usually necessary if you have only a single whelping female and she is going to have the pups indoors. The whelping box should be lined with several layers of clean newspaper at the time of delivery. You can use clean sheets or towels as well, but newspapers are easier to remove and discard during delivery.

WHELPING BOX

If you have a long-haired dog, you may wish to gently clip (not shave) the hair away from the vulva and nipples before delivery. It makes delivery a little more tidy and makes it a little easier for the newborn pups to find the nipples, but is not a real necessity.

Delivery

About five days before the expected date of *parturition* (delivery) you may start taking your dog's temperature morning and evening. At the onset of the *first stage* of labor, the rectal temperature will drop transiently and markedly from the normal of about 101 to 102.5 to as low as ninety-eight degrees F. At this time, or sometimes earlier, the female will lose her appetite and seek the nest box. Vomiting is a possibility. If you have failed to adjust her to the whelping area, your female may try to nest on your bed, in a closet, or in some other unsuitable spot. Take her back to the whelping box and stay with her until she becomes comfortable in the area. During the first stage of labor the female shreds and tears at the bedding and may even pull hair from her body in her attempt to make a nest. Panting and trembling are often seen and her pulse rate will increase. Colostrum may drip from the nipples. Uterine contractions moving the pup from the uterine horn to the body of the uterus and cervix are occuring during this first stage, which may last twelve to twenty-four hours. A long first stage is particularly characteristic of a first pregnancy. If the signs last twenty-five hours or longer, or your dog seems to pass into the second stage then back to the first, or seems usually uncomfortable, discuss the matter with your veterinarian before assuming everything is all right.

During the *second stage* of labor you will see forceful straining movements caused by the simultaneous contractions of the abdominal muscles and diaphragm. At the beginning of this stage you *may* see a small amount of straw-colored fluid passed at the vulva. This is due to the rupture of the *allantois-chorion* which covers the puppy as it passes into the vaginal canal. It may take as long as an hour for a pup to be

WHELPING

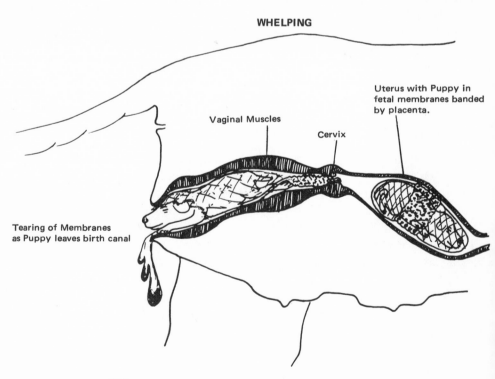

Uterus with Puppy in fetal membranes banded by placenta.

Vaginal Muscles

Cervix

Tearing of Membranes as Puppy leaves birth canal

200

delivered once the second stage begins. The female may lie on her side or on her sternum. Some females stand and squat as if they were going to have a bowel movement during the most vigorous portions of straining. The *amnion* (membranous sac) enclosing the head of the puppy sometimes appears at the vulva. It may, however, be ruptured before the pup is delivered. Once the head and paws of the puppy appear, complete delivery should be finished within fifteen minutes — if not, call your veterinarian. The nose and feet of the puppy should not appear and disappear each time the female strains. In the classic birth position the puppy is delivered with its sternum on the vaginal floor, nose first and its front paws along the sides of its face. Thirty to forty per cent of pups, however, are delivered rear legs first. This usually causes no problem.

As soon as the puppy is delivered, the amnionic sac (amnion) should be broken to allow the puppy to breathe. Inexperienced or nervous females may not do this. If this is the case, you must break the amnion or the puppy will suffocate. If the umbilical cord is not broken during delivery, it is not necessary to break it immediately. Significant amounts of blood are found in the placenta, and by allowing the umbilical cord to remain unbroken, you give time for this blood to pass into the pup. Normally the mother nips the umbilical cord and breaks it as she cleans and licks the puppy following delivery. If she doesn't, a clean piece of thread or unwaxed dental floss should be tied around the cord about one inch from the body wall. Then cut or break the cord just beyond (*distal to*) the tie.

TIED UMBILICAL CORD

Normally the placenta (afterbirth) is delivered with or just after the puppy. It is a good idea to count the placentas as they are delivered to be sure all are passed. Retained placentas can cause uterine inflammation and infection (see page 143). It is normal, but unnecessary, for the female to eat the placenta following each delivery. It is best to let the bitch eat only one or two; the ingestion of too many can cause vomiting and diarrhea. The time of delivery of the placenta and the period of uterine rest that follows is the *third stage* of labor. During the rest period the bitch usually lies still and tends her pups. Some will get up and take a drink of water. The rest period between puppies varies from ten to fifteen minutes to several hours. It is not usually more than one or two hours however. An average time for delivery of four or five pups would be six to eight hours, although normal parturitions may last up to twenty-four or even thirty-six hours.

Difficult Delivery (Dystocia)

Difficult deliveries are usually caused by obstruction to delivery of the fetus, or uterine inertia (see page 203). *Dystocia* must usually be treated with the help of a veterinarian. If any of the stages of labor seem abnormally long or if your dog shows signs of excessive discomfort, call your veterinarian.

If you can see a puppy at the vulva, but its delivery seems slow or it appears and disappears, you may be able to help deliver it. Wash your hands and lubricate a finger with a lubricant, like petroleum or K-Y® jelly. Insert your finger into the vaginal canal and move it around the puppy, trying to determine where the head and front and rear legs are. You may be able to hook a front leg in an abnormal backward position and bring it forward. If the puppy seems fairly normally placed, grasp it with a gauze pad, cloth, or your fingers, and gently pull with each contraction. It is best to try to grasp the pup around the shoulders to avoid excessive pressure on the head, and it is best to pull downward because the vagina is angled towards the ground. Do not pull on the amnionic sac surrounding the puppy. If the pup's head just seems too big to fit through the vulva, you can sometimes gently manipulate the edges of the vulva around the head. A veterinarian will sometimes make an incision at the upper part of the vulva to deliver a pup stuck at the bottom of the birth canal. This cut through the tissue *(episiotomy)* allows the vulvar opening to enlarge. I would advise you not to do this, unless it is impossible to get veterinary help.

If a retained placenta blocks delivery of a pup, you can often reach it. Grasp it with a gauze pad or cloth and gently but firmly pull until it passes out of the vaginal canal. Once an obstruction to delivery is relieved, a female will often have a prolonged rest period before the next puppy is delivered.

Failure of the uterus to contract efficiently *(uterine inertia)* may occur following prolonged straining to deliver a pup or may be primary as in the case of an obese, underexercised or older dog. A form of uterine inertia can be caused by excessive excitement, or by other psychological stresses during delivery. This is why it is important to familiarize your dog with the whelping area well before delivery. It is also why strangers should not be present during delivery. A labor inhibited by psychogenic stresses can often be helped by having only one or two familiar people remain with the dog during delivery.

If no obstruction to delivery is found, your veterinarian may have to administer a drug called *oxytocin* to initiate new uterine contractions. Other drugs may be administered as well. If medical therapy does not initiate proper birth or there is some other problem which cannot be relieved with external manipulations, your veterinarian will want to perform a *caesarian section* — in which the puppies are removed through an incision in the abdomen. It is usually possible to spay your female at the time of such surgery. Unless the difficult birth is solely attributable to the puppies, it is probably best to have the spay. Mothers who have difficult births tend to repeat themselves. Most bitches are able to nurse and care for their puppies normally following caesarian section.

Puppies That Won't Breathe

If the bitch doesn't break the amnionic sac covering the puppy's head within a minute or two, you should. Hold the puppy in your hands or wrap it in a towel. Support the head so it doesn't swing freely, then move the whole puppy vigorously in a wide arch from about

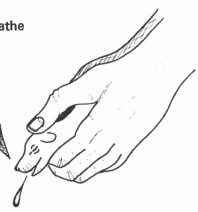

SHAKING NEWBORN PUP TO CLEAR FLUIDS FROM MOUTH

chest to knee level. At the end of the arc the pup's nose should point toward the ground. This helps clear excess fluids from the nose and major airways. Other methods to remove excess fluids are to put your mouth over the puppy's nose and mouth and suck or to use an infant ear syringe to suck the fluid from the puppy's mouth and throat. After clearing the airways, rub the chest and body of the puppy with a rough towel. If the pup still does not start to breathe and cry, take in a breath of air, place your mouth over the pup's nose and mouth and blow gently until you see the chest expand. Remove your mouth and let the puppy exhale, then repeat. Shaking and towel drying even healthy puppies is a good idea if the mother is not interested or is too slow.

Care of the Female Following Delivery

Within twenty-four hours following parturition it is advisable to take the mother and pups to a veterinarian for examination. At this time she can be palpated to determine whether all the pups have been delivered, and an injection of oxytocin can be given which will cause the uterus to contract — expelling excess fluids and any placenta which may remain. This also stimulates milk letdown. The veterinarian can also examine the pups for abnormalities. (If the pups are to have cosmetic surgery, page 209, wait to bring them in for examination until that time.)

A large amount of dark green, mucoid material called *lochia* is discharged from the vulva following the delivery. Within a week this discharge normally changes to a small amount of odorless brown or reddish material. Within another week, the discharge is usually clear mucus. If discharges persist beyond fourteen to twenty days, are odorous, abnormal in amount or look like pus or blood, do not wait further. Take your dog to a veterinarian for a thorough examination.

Within twenty-four hours following delivery your dog should be normally interested in eating and drinking. The first few days her diet can be the same as that preceding delivery. As lactation progresses, the rule of thumb is to feed the normal maintenance requirement *plus* 100 calories per day per pound of puppies. As in pregnancy, protein requirements for lactation are higher than normal maintenance levels. By the end of lactation a female may be consuming three times as much food as she was before breeding. Again however, the best guide is the appearance of the dog. If she is looking thin and "worn out" her diet may need adjustment. Balanced vitamin-mineral supplements are probably most beneficial when used during lactation.

Problems Following Parturition

The common problems affecting the female following parturition are infection of the uterus *(acute metritis)*, inflammation of mammary glands *(mastitis)*, and milk fever *(puerperal tetany)*. These problems are covered in Diagnostic Medicine pages 143, and 113 and Emergency Medicine page 159.

Care of Orphan Puppies

Many new mothers who need help with the first care of their newly delivered puppies care for them successfully later. So don't worry too much if your dog seems a clumsy mother at first. First time mothers may not have much milk during the first twenty-four hours. This too is not cause for concern unless it continues. Dogs which ignore or actively reject their litters may be helped by tranquilizers which your veterinarian can prescribe. In some of these cases, however, and in cases where the female dies, you must take the mother's place. A normal litter is quiet, and the puppies sleep most of the time when not nursing. Puppies which cry and squirm continually should alert you to look for signs of neglect or illness such as weakness, inability to nurse, diarrhea or lowered body temperature. (See below.) If you find signs of illness, have the litter examined by a veterinarian, since treating very young puppies is difficult.

Puppy's Age In Days	Normal Rectal Temperature (F)
1	92-97
2	95-98
5	96-98
7	96-98
14	97-98
21	98-99
28	99-101

If at all possible, the puppies should suckle the first milk or colostrum. It is rich in antibodies which can protect the puppies against disease during the first weeks of their life. Puppies are best able to absorb these special proteins through their intestine for twenty-four to thirty-six hours after birth.

Puppies which must be separated from their mothers must be kept in a warm environment free from drafts because they have difficulty controlling their body temperature. From birth to about five days of age the room or box temperature should be eight-five to ninety degrees F; from about five to twenty days about eighty degrees F. After twenty days the environmental temperature should be lowered gradually to somewhere between seventy and seventy-five degrees F by the fourth week. The best way to provide the proper temperature for orphan puppies, if you don't have a human or poultry incubator, is to use an electric heating pad. Hang the heating pad down one side of the box and onto about one-fourth of the bottom. Then adjust the temperature control to maintain the proper air temperature. By covering only part of the floor you allow the puppies to get away from the heat if necessary. The heating pad and box bottom should be covered with newspaper or cloth which is changed each time it becomes soiled. Most authorities recommend that each puppy be kept in a separate compartment until two or three weeks old to prevent them from sucking each others ears, tails, feet and genitals, but if they are allowed to suckle sufficiently at each nursing period, you will probably find that this is not necessary.

Research indicates that puppies handled daily are more emotionally stable and resistant to stress. This does not mean, however, that children should handle them without direction or that they should be handled by strangers (who can carry disease). Expect the dried umbilical cord to fall off a normal puppy two to three days following birth. Eyes open around twelve to fifteen days of age, and the ear canals open about two days later.

Feeding Orphan Puppies   Orphan puppies should be fed the formula that most approaches the composition of normal bitches' milk. Although you can get by with home formulas made from cows' milk, commercial formulas (e.g., Orphalac®, Esbilac®, Havolac®), available in pet stores and from some veterinarians come much closer to the real thing. These formulas can be used to supplement feed large litters as well. The best way to determine how much formula each puppy needs is to weigh the puppy and use a table of calorie requirements. The required amount of formula is then divided into three portions fed at eight hour intervals.

Calories (Kilocalories) Needed Daily/Pound	Age in Weeks
about 60	1
about 70	2
about 80 to 90	3
more than 90	4+

(Example: A 225 gram (one-half pound) puppy needs ½ x 60 = 30 Calories per day during the first week of life. About one ounce (30 ml) formula containing one Calorie per milliliter.)

If you supply the proper caloric requirements you do not need to feed a puppy more than three times a day. However, if the puppy cannot take in the required volume at three feedings, the number of feedings must be increased. At each feeding the puppy should eat until just comfortably full — not until the abdomen is tight and distended. A steady weight gain and a normal stool are indicators that the puppy is being properly fed.

Home Formulas for Orphan Pups			
Evaporated milk	4 oz.	Whole cow's milk	26.5 oz.
Water	4 oz.	Cream (12% fat)	6.5 oz.
Karo syrup	½ oz.	Egg yolk	1
Egg yolk	1	Bone meal	6 gm.
Halibut liver oil	2 drops	Citric acid	4 gm.
Thiamine		Vitamin A	2,000 I.U.
hydrochloride	1 mg	Vitamin D	500 I.U.
About 30 calories per ounce		About 38 calories per ounce	

All formula is best fed after warming to body temperature (about 100 degrees F). Formula can be administered with an eye dropper, syringe, nursing bottle or stomach tube. A nursing bottle and anticolic nipple are usually easiest and safest in inexperienced hands. The holes in the nipple should be enlarged if the formula does not drip slowly from the nipple when the full bottle is inverted. Be sure the nipple size is suitable for the size puppy you are trying to nurse. Hold the puppy on its stomach. Gently separate the lips with your fingers and slip the nipple in. A healthy hungry puppy will usually suck vigorously after tasting the milk. Use of a towel will give the puppy some- thing to push and knead against as if nursing naturally. Weak pups may have to be held vertically and formula placed slowly in their mouths. DO NOT place a puppy on its back to feed it or squirt liquid rapidly into its mouth. These methods can cause aspiration of the fluid into the lungs,

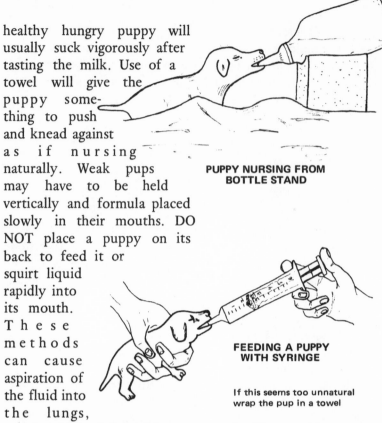

PUPPY NURSING FROM BOTTLE STAND

FEEDING A PUPPY WITH SYRINGE

If this seems too unnatural wrap the pup in a towel

which will be followed by pneumonia. If you wish to use a stomach tube for feeding (the fastest method), ask your veterinarian for a demonstration.

After each feeding the puppies should be stimulated to urinate and defecate. Moisten a cotton swab, tissue or soft cloth with warm water and gently, but vigorously, massage the ano-genital area. Nursing puppies' stools are normally firm (not hard) and yellow. If diarrhea develops the first thing to do is dilute the formula by about one-half by the addition of boiled water. If this does not help within twenty-four hours, consult a veterinarian. Feeding cows milk often causes diarrhea because of its high lactose content.

Weaning

Between the ages of two and three weeks you can start to wean most puppies. Place a shallow pan of formula on the floor of their pen. At first the puppies will step and fall into it and make a general mess, but soon they will be lapping at it. When this stage is reached, high protein pablum, meat baby food or puppy chow can be added to make a gruel. After they are eating the gruel, the amount of formula can be decreased until they are eating solid food and drinking water. Eggs, cottage cheese, yogurt and meat may be added to their diet as they become adjusted to eating solid food. All changes in feeding should be made gradually to avoid causing digestive upsets. Puppies with a natural mother should be allowed to continue nursing during the weaning process, until they are eating well-balanced meals of solid food on their own. During this time the mother may sometimes regurgitate food in front of her puppies. This is a normal part of the natural weaning process and is no cause for worry.

By five weeks of age puppies have most of their baby teeth, so that the mother will usually become more and more reluctant to nurse. As the puppies increase their intake of solid food, you should decrease the mother's intake of food and gradually restrict nursing time. Weaning may be achieved completely this way, but if there is an actual weaning day offer the bitch water but withhold food, or feed only a small portion of the maintenance diet on that day. Over the following five days gradually increase food back to the normal maintenance level. This procedure helps decrease her milk production.

If milk production does not seem to decrease rapidly enough and the female seems uncomfortable, DO NOT remove milk from the glands. This will only prolong the problem. Cold packs applied to the mammary glands may help, as may camphor oil. If the problem is severe consult a veterinarian for help.

Cosmetic Surgery

Removal of the dewclaws, part of the tail *(docking)* and part of the ear *(cropping)* are surgical procedures performed mainly for cosmetic reasons. Dewclaws are often loosely attached and tend to become caught and torn. This is a particular problem in hunting dogs and dogs which roam in the country. Removal of dewclaws and tail docking should be done by your veterinarian during the first week of life (three days of age is best) when anesthesia is not necessary and the surgery is the least traumatic. Which dewclaws are to be

Dewclaw Removal, Tail Docking, Ear Cropping

209

removed and how much of the tail to remove varies with the breed standards. If you have mixed breed puppies or do not plan to sell your purebred puppies for show purposes, you may choose not to have the tails docked but just to have the dewclaws removed.

The optimal time for ear cropping varies with the breed, but is usually around nine weeks of age. This is purely a cosmetic procedure. I feel it should only be done if the puppy is going to be shown. Although some puppies seem to experience little discomfort following ear cropping, many are extremely uncomfortable. In order to get many types of ears to stand you must work seriously for weeks with various types of taping and supporting materials — an "ordeal" for both you and your puppy. In Canada and England dogs are shown without cropped ears. If veterinarians and owners in the United States would refuse to crop dogs' ears, the breed standards could be changed and this unnecessary surgical procedure could be abandoned.

Umbilical Hernias

A *hernia* is a protrusion of a part of the body or an organ through an abnormal opening of the surrounding tissues. A common hernia occuring in dogs is the umbilical hernia, in which a portion of fat or internal organs protrudes through an incompletely closed umbilical ring. Most umbilical hernias are present at birth, but some may be acquired if the mother chews the umbilical cord too short or through other careless handling of the cord. Umbilical hernias in dogs are usually small, often get smaller as the puppy ages, and usually do not require surgical repair. If your puppies have large umbilical hernias or hernias that you can push into the abdomen with your finger, consult your veterinarian about the necessity of repair.

Pustular Dermatitis

Pustular dermatitis is an infection of the skin of young puppies usually caused by *staphlococci* bacteria. You may first notice crusts or scabs which are sticking the hairs together or a wet and sticky area of skin. These areas are often on the head or neck, but may be anywhere on the body. If you look closely over the puppy's body, you may see small red or pus-filled bumps. If you don't notice these early skin changes, you may first see a large swelling in the *ventral* (under the neck region) or sometimes one or more swellings occur alone. This is usually a sign of infection and of abscessation of lymph nodes in the areas, and needs immediate veterinary attention. Abscesses must usually be opened and drained (see page 109). Daily gentle cleansing of the affected areas with Phisohex® or other antiseptic soap followed by *thorough* rinsing may be sufficient to control localized skin infections. Usually washing should be combined with antibiotics prescribed by your veterinarian.

If you need more information on breeding and reproduction the following book may be helpful:

Hansen, J.S., *How to Breed and Whelp Dogs,* Charles C. Thomas, Publisher, Springfield, Illinois, 1972.

How To Sex Puppies

MALE

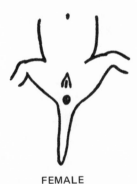

FEMALE

You, Your Dog and
Your Veterinarian

You, Your Dog and Your Veterinarian

Choosing a veterinarian is one of the most important decisions you will have to make concerning your dog's health. There are bad veterinarians as well as good ones, just as in any profession. I can offer no specific rules for finding

How To Find A "Good" Veterinarian

the best one for your dog. However, considering some of the following things may help you in your search.

Find a veterinarian you feel comfortable with. No matter how skilled the veterinarian, you cannot make best use of the services of someone you dislike personally or feel uncomfortable being around.

A good veterinarian explains things thoroughly and in a manner you can understand. There is a shortage of veterinarians in the United States; this puts great demands on their time. Because of this your veterinarian may sometimes seem rushed or fail to explain things thoroughly to you. I think this is understandable, but if it happens and you are disturbed about it, let your veterinarian know. There is no

need to give explanations in totally technical terms. Medical terminology is more exact, but can be confusing so most things should be explained in general terms that you can understand. Veterinarians who rely continually on technical language when discussing your dog's health may be on an "ego trip" or trying to "snow" you, but, because they are so familiar with medical terms sometimes it's that they forget you aren't. Let your veterinarian know you are having trouble understanding them, and request an attempt to have things explained more simply. A good veterinarian will appreciate a polite request.

Good and bad veterinarians exist in all age groups. Don't fall into the trap that an older veterinarian knows more and a younger one less, or vice versa. In general, veterinarians who have been in practice for a while have more experience, but remember, not everyone learns from experience. A recent graduate often has better knowledge of new techniques available, but may seem clumsy or insecure. Keep these things in mind, and try to evaluate your veterinarian on the quality of care they give your pet. The best veterinarians are continually improving their skills through continuing education as they practice.

One way to evaluate a new veterinarian is through your first office call. You should see the veterinarian personally,

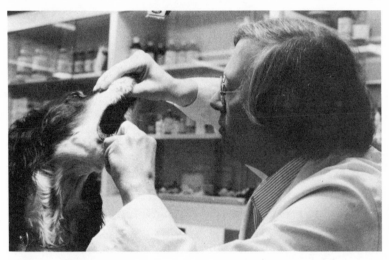

not be required to leave your dog and "check back later" or have lay help take care of the whole problem. The people who handle your pet, both assistants and veterinarian, should seem capable and use a minimum of restraint on nervous animals unless they have made an attempt to "make friends" without success. A thorough physical examination should be performed and questions regarding your dog's medical history should be asked. Unless your dog sees the veterinarian extremely frequently, a general physical should always be performed at each visit. (Since dogs can't tell us their problems we have to look for them.)

A clean office and new equipment are often indicative of good veterinary care. But don't be misled by a fancy "front room." Most good veterinarians will allow you to see the whole hospital *at a convenient time.* One who won't may have something to hide. Some veterinarians have fancy equipment, but don't use it or use it improperly. Veterinarians in small towns or rural areas may not have enough demand to necessitate expensive specialized equipment in their offices. Again, try to judge your veterinarian on the kind of medicine practiced, not on appearances.

It is as difficult to judge a veterinarian by their fees as it is according to the kind of equipment in their office. What is a reasonable fee varies between geographical areas and types of practices. In general, it is "fair" to expect to pay more for veterinary services at hospitals where the latest equipment and specialized services are available, since it costs the veterinarian more to maintain such services. (Remember, most veterinarians, unlike physicians, don't have large central hospitals for patients who need special care and so must maintain their own.) If you are concerned about the fee, be sure to ask your veterinarian about it if they don't bring up the matter first.

Veterinarians who don't maintain specialized equipment must refer some cases. A good veterinarian recognizes their limitations. Veterinarians who won't make referrals when requested may be trying to hide their own inadequacies.

Choose a veterinary clinic which provides emergency service or will be able to refer you to emergency care when necessary. Some communities have central emergency services which work closely with the local veterinarians; others do not. Find out what your veterinarian or the community provides while your dog is healthy so you won't waste precious time when a true emergency arises.

How To Be A "Good" Client
Once you have found a veterinarian who seems capable and interested in providing your pet with good health care, you can do even more to assure that your dog is treated well. Like other people, veterinarians are inclined to provide the

best service to people who are nice to them ("good clients"). Since veterinarians are people and as such aren't infallible or tireless, they appreciate consideration on your part. If you keep a few simple courtesies in mind and try to practice them. These signs of appreciation will make most veterinarians respond with their best efforts.

If your veterinarian takes appointments, try to be on time. This helps keep the veterinarian on schedule and helps

prevent a long wait for others. Avoid "dropping in" with your dog without an appointment; call ahead if you have a sick pet and cannot wait another day. Never drop in for routine preventive care such as vaccination or deworming unless your veterinarian chooses not to use an appointment system. And when you do come in be sure to bring your dog on a leash or in your arms to prevent mishaps and disturbances in the waiting room.

Avoid dropping your dog off for care unless your veterinarian specifically directs you to. Most people would never consider dropping their child off at the pediatrician's, but many seem to expect that veterinarians should provide "one hour, one stop" service and get good results. Your dog usually receives better care if you discuss the problem with your veterinarian as the examination is performed. If your animal is very sick and it is impossible for you to wait for an office call, call ahead and discuss the problem with the veterinarian first. They may be able to advise you on home treatment, and, at least, be able to deal with the problem more calmly than if you show up in a rush hoping to leave your pet.

Do not disturb your veterinarian at night, on holidays or their other time off for non-emergency matters. If you have any doubts about the emergency nature of an illness, call, but don't call just for general information.

Don't expect your veterinarian to make a diagnosis over the phone, or solely on the basis of a physical examination. And don't expect the veterinary clinic to be a drug store, supplying drugs on demand. Competent veterinarians interested in your dog's health want to examine your pet and may require laboratory tests before prescribing drugs or making a diagnosis no matter how sure you are of the diagnosis. They do this not "to hassle" you, but to protect your dog as well as themselves. Don't feel that you can't even call your veterinarian for advice, however. Just be prepared with some solid facts. If you can tell your veterinarian whether or not your dog has a fever, what are the basic signs of illness or injury, and how long they have been present, they will probably be willing to give you some help over the telephone in spite of a busy schedule. If you can't supply such information, though, don't be surprised if you are told that it is impossible to help you over the telephone.

Don't let signs persist for several days without or in spite of home care before consulting a veterinarian. It is extremely frustrating for a veterinarian to see an animal die of an illness which could have been treated successfully if professional care had begun sooner. And, once you have consulted a veterinarian, please follow their directions. It is quite irritating to have someone complain that a treatment didn't work only to find out later that the medication was not used, or used improperly. If you are having trouble, notify your veterinarian, but don't stop treatment without their advice.

Learn to use your veterinarian as a resource for your animal's health. Know that help is there when you need it, but use this book, your patience and your common sense (intuition) to take most of the responsibility for your dog's health. This book is intended as a tool to help you determine the limits of your responsibility and when you should draw on the veterinarian's resources. By using it this way you will be practicing preventive medicine and may forestall illness and extra medical costs before they develop. Remember your relationship to your dog, your moods and your attitude toward their health and well-being are vital factors in their health and the effectiveness of your veterinarian. If you can temper your concern for your animal with an intuitive understanding of them and with the knowledge you have gained about health care, you will avoid needless emotional upset and promote the growth of the three way relationship of health — you, your dog, and your veterinarian.

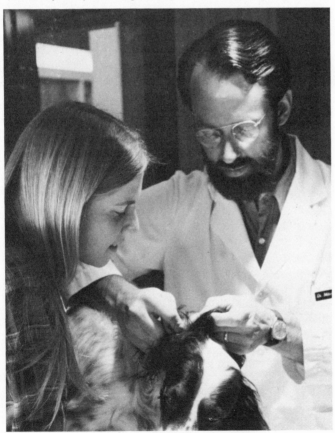

Writing this book has been both a chore and a pleasure. Although I had planned on being a veterinarian as long as I can remember (even before I learned that "animal doctors" are called veterinarians), I had never considered writing a book. In fact, I was more than a little grateful that my trip through veterinary school (U.C. Davis) included only one genuine term paper. Last year, though, things changed when I met Don Gerrard, publisher of Bookworks and, fortunately for me, a client of the bay area clinic where I practice. He suggested that I write a book on dog and cat care. I was reluctant at first because of my distaste for writing, but the idea was intriguing. After talking with Don and looking over other Bookworks books which had taken new directions, I decided that a new kind of book on dog care was needed and agreed to try to write one. The next step was finding an illustrator. Again I was lucky; I found out that Tom Reed, a good friend and a veterinarian also, could draw. What could be better than if he would agree to do the illustrations? And he did.

223

Then the real work began. As with most things, looking back, the pleasure stands out and the pain is dull; but I can remember several times wishing that I'd never agreed to undertake such a project. Over the year I was alternately elated and depressed. Now I'm feeling happy and full of thanks, which I'd like to express to all the people who helped me with the manuscript — George Ahlgren, Ian Dunbar, Nancy Ehrlich, Michael Floyd, Jay Fuller, Jim and Sandy Lane, Helen Root, Cindy and Layton Smith and, especially, Don and Tom. Kent Rush also deserves special thanks for her work on the cover design. I hope the sum of our work, The Well Dog Book, *is useful to you, and I would like to hear from you, your feelings pro and con, about it. I won't be able to answer specific questions about dog health care, but send your other questions and suggestions to me at:*

1550 Solano Avenue
Albany, California 94706

For those of you who own cats, this book's companion volume, The Well Cat Book, *is published by Random House/ Bookworks.*

Terri McGinnis

224

General Index

226

Burns, chemical 158
     electric 157
     heat (thermal) 157

Caesarian section 193, 203

Cancer (see Tumors)

Calcium in diet 55, 56, 59–60

Callus 111

Capillary filling time 32, 145

Carbohydrates, in diet 57–58

Carry dog, how to 144

Castration 193

Cataracts 161

Chewing 44

Cheyletiella mites 90

Chiggers 90

Chills (see Shivering)

Chlorophyll tablets 189

Circulatory system 31–33 (see also Blood, Heart)

Coat (see Hair)

Cod liver oil, in diet 60

Colostrum 66, 206

Conjunctivitis 81, 104, 114

Constipation 134–135

Contact dermatitis 85, 105–106

Convulsions 68, 76, 110, 144, 151–152, 153, 159

Corticosteroids 181

Cosmetic surgery 209–210

Coprophagy 136

Cough 69, 78, 82, 120, 157, 164

Cryptorchid 27, 193

Cutaneous larval migrans 80

Cuts (see Wounds)

Cystitis 141–142

Dandruff 58, 90, 104, 112

Deafness 161

Death, signs of 149

Dehydration, signs of 98
     treatment of 99

C

D

227

F

Foreign bodies, in ear 48, 117
    in eye 115
    in digestive tract 132, 134
    in mouth 118
    in nose 121
    in skin 48, 110

Foxtails (see Plant awns)

Fracture, signs of 123, 124
    splinting of 123–124
    treatment for 125

Fungus (see Ringworm)

G **Gagging** 118, 120

Gastritis 131

Gastroenteritis 132

Gastrointestinal tract (see Digestive system)

Genital organs (see Reproductive organs)

Geriatric, diet 63, 160
    exercise 160
    medicine 160–166

Grass eating 131

Grooming 45–52

Gums, care of 62
    inflammation of (gingivitis) 52, 119
    normal appearance 22
    pale 22, 71, 79, 83, 86, 145
    receding 52
    red 22, 52

H **Hair**, care of 45–48
    kinds of 17
    loss of (including shedding) 17, 85, 88, 89, 104, 105, 106, 111
    mats in 48, 135
    normal appearance 17–18
    paint in 48
    tar in 18

Head shaking 87, 117, 118

Head tilt 117, 118

Hearing, loss of 161
    test for 161

Heart, anatomy of 31
    disease 163–164
    external massage 150–151
    failure 163–164
    how to examine 31–32
    murmur 163
    rate 31–32
    worms 81–82

I

Nose, blood from 121, 147
        cool 15
        discharge from 30, 69, 104, 118, 120
        foreign object in 121
        how to examine 15, 30
        normal appearance 15,30
        thickened skin of 69, 118
        warm 15

Nutrition (see also Food) 53—63

Nursing at home 169—174

Obedience training 39, 41

Obesity 61, 138—139, 189

OFA (Orthopedic Foundation for Animals) 127

Orphan puppies, care of 205—208

Osteoarthritis 127, 161—162

Otitis externa 116—118

Ovariohysterectomy 189—192

Pain (see Index of Signs)

Paralysis (see Index of Signs)

Parasites, external 83—91
        diagnosis of 72—73
        internal 73—83

Parturition, care of female after 204—205
        difficult 196, 202—203
        normal 199—202

Penis, normal appearance of 28
        inflammation of 140

Phosphorus in diet 55, 56, 59—60

Physical examination 7—8, 35—36

Physiology, definition of 7

Pills, how to administer 170—172

Pinworms 82

Placenta, eating 201
        retained 143, 201, 202

Plant awns 48

Pneumonia 69, 78, 120, 134, 208

Pododermatitis 106

Poisoning, general treatment of 153
        plant 155
        salmon 74
        snail bait 152
        strychnine 152—153
        table of 154

O

P

233

234

T

V

W